At Issue

How Does Religion Influence Politics?

Other Books in the At Issue Series:

At Issue

How Does Religion Influence Politics?

Stefan Kiesbye, Book Editor

GREENHAVEN PRESS
A part of Gale, Cengage Learning

GALE
CENGAGE Learning

Detroit • New York • San Francisco • New Haven, Conn • Waterville, Maine • London

GALE
CENGAGE Learning™

Christine Nasso, *Publisher*
Elizabeth Des Chenes, *Managing Editor*

© 2010 Greenhaven Press, a part of Gale, Cengage Learning.

Gale and Greenhaven Press are registered trademarks used herein under license.

For more information, contact:
Greenhaven Press
27500 Drake Rd.
Farmington Hills, MI 48331-3535
Or you can visit our Internet site at gale.cengage.com

For product information and technology assistance, contact us at

Gale Customer Support, 1-800-877-4253
For permission to use material from this text or product, submit all requests online at www.cengage.com/permissions

Further permissions questions can be emailed to permissionrequest@cengage.com

Articles in Greenhaven Press anthologies are often edited for length to meet page requirements. In addition, original titles of these works are changed to clearly present the main thesis and to explicitly indicate the author's opinion. Every effort is made to ensure that Greenhaven Press accurately reflects the original intent of the authors. Every effort has been made to trace the owners of copyrighted material.

Cover image created by Andrew Judd/© 1999–2009 Masterfile Corporation. All rights reserved.

LIBRARY OF CONGRESS CATALOGING-IN-PUBLICATION DATA

How does religion influence politics? / Stefan Kiesbye, book editor.
    p. cm. -- (At issue)
    Includes bibliographical references and index.
    ISBN 978-0-7377-4675-4 (hardcover) -- ISBN 978-0-7377-4676-1 (pbk.)
    1. Religion and politics--United States. 2. United States--Religion. I. Kiesbye, Stefan.
    BL2525.H678 2010
    261.70973--dc22

                                                                          2009046720

Printed in the United States of America
2 3 4 5 6 7 14 13 12 11 10

Contents

Introduction

On February 25, 1990, 26-year-old Terri Schiavo collapsed in her St. Petersburg, Florida, apartment due to respiratory and cardiac arrest. Her husband Michael called 911, and when paramedics arrived, Schiavo was unconscious, had no pulse, and was not breathing. Despite efforts by hospital staff, the lack of oxygen had already severely damaged her brain, and Schiavo was in a coma. When Schiavo came out of her coma after two and a half months, she was in a persistent vegetative state (PVS) and was kept alive through a feeding tube.

Doctors gave her an extremely minimal chance of recovery, and even with hospital care and experimental treatment at the University of California, San Francisco, Schiavo's condition did not show any improvement.

What started as a private tragedy slowly became a public battleground. In 1998, after eight years of failed treatments and against the wishes of Schiavo's parents, Robert and Mary Schindler, Michael Schiavo filed a petition to have Schiavo's feeding tube removed. He held the position that his wife could not regain her cognitive functions and should not be kept alive through artificial means. During the next years, Michael and the Schindlers battled in court over that petition. After the Schindlers' motions in the case had been dismissed by numerous judges, in 2003 the Florida House and Senate became involved, passing "Terri's Law." The law enabled the governor, Jeb Bush, to issue a stay (which temporarily suspends the order of the court) in cases like Schiavo's. Once signed into law, Governor Bush immediately issued a stay, and Schiavo's feeding tube was restored. The law was struck down in 2004, however, as unconstitutional, and after several months of legal maneuvering Schiavo's feeding tube was again ordered removed by the judge, who ruled that the feeding tube should be removed March 18, 2005. In March 2005, the case attracted the attention of the national media when President George W. Bush signed federal legislation to transfer the jurisdiction of the case to federal courts.

As the *St. Petersburg Times* wrote, on December 20, 2005, "Her parents, Bob and Mary Schindler, fought [Michael Schiavo] bitterly, but in February [of 2005] it appeared he would finally prevail: A Pinellas County [Florida] judge ruled that her feeding tube could be disconnected on March 18. In Washington, Republican leaders and conservative activists were outraged. To some who watched a video of Schiavo shot in her hospice room, it appeared that she could follow a balloon, that she reacted to her mother's voice. That sometimes, she smiled. How could they let her die? . . . Then-House Majority Leader Tom DeLay quickly took charge of the bill in the House. [Then-Senator Rick] Santorum and Majority Leader Bill Frist, R-Tenn., took over in the Senate. The politicians who styled themselves as Schiavo's saviors denounced those who would let her die as evil, as heartless, as killers."

Many critics contend that the Terri Schiavo case clearly blurred the line between religion and politics. In a March 2005 speech, Tom DeLay said, "It is more than just Terri Schiavo. This is a critical issue for people in this position, and it is also a critical issue to fight that fight for life, whether it be euthanasia or abortion. I tell you, ladies and gentlemen, one thing God has brought to us is Terri Schiavo to elevate the visibility of what's going on in America. That Americans would be so barbaric as to pull a feeding tube out of a person that is lucid and starve them to death for two weeks. . . ." The political posturing worked, and legislation was passed to give federal courts jurisdiction over the case, thus allowing the Schindlers' a new forum to appeal.

Former Republican Senator John Danforth, in his book *Faith and Politics*, takes a critical view of the proceedings that inserted government into the private lives of citizens and writes that, "Republican leaders gladly abandoned principles that for decades had bound their party together in order to meet the demands of Christian conservatives . . . The sad case of Terri Schiavo convinced me of the Christian Right's dominance in the Republican Party." In his words, the President's intervention on Schiavo's behalf was in an effort to "satisfy the demands of their political base: the Christian Right."

The *St. Petersburg Times* agrees with his observation, but contends that, "After four years of galloping triumph for the conservative Republican agenda, the rush to pass Schiavo legislation marked a critical turning point in Washington, helping expand fissures in a Republican Party known for discipline, emboldening Democrats and derailing conservative social initiatives that had been expected to win easy approval in Congress this year [2005]."

Despite the change to federal jurisdiction, like the Florida appeals, further appeals from the Schindlers were denied. The decision to have the feeding tube removed was carried out on March 18, and Terri Schiavo died on March 31, 2005. The Schiavo case is not only notorious as a case concerning the many ethical issues surrounding euthanasia and end of life decisions; it also has, to many observers, become an example of the often complex intersection of religion and politics.

1

Religion Cannot Be Separated from Politics

Richard John Neuhaus

Richard John Neuhaus was a Catholic priest, and founder of First Things, *a journal covering religion and politics.*

It is not possible to exclude religion from political discourse. Not only is it impossible, but to attempt to do so is undemocratic. The founding fathers sought not to separate religion from politics, but to ensure that politics would not encroach on religion. At the heart of all political debates is a moral question, and religious convictions as well as non religious, but still moral, convictions play an integral role in those debates.

*L*ast Saturday [November 10, 2007], the British magazine *The Economist sponsored a debate on this resolution: "Religion and politics should always be kept separate." There was an audience of about a thousand, and at the beginning of the debate the vote was about five to one in favor of the resolution. This is Manhattan, after all. At the end of the debate the house was pretty evenly divided but still with a slight majority in favor. . . .*

Herewith my opening statement at the debate. The connections between religion and politics is a huge subject and, in First Things *and elsewhere, I have addressed other dimensions of the question. But this was tailored to an audience assumed, correctly, to be strongly hostile to the argument. And the house was turned around, almost. You might perhaps find the statement of some interest.*

Favoring a Separation of Church and State

I speak in favor of the separation of church and state, and therefore against the resolution that religion and politics should always be kept separate. Permit me to explain. To enforce the exclusion of religion from politics, or from public life more generally, violates the First Amendment guarantee of the "free exercise of religion." The free exercise of religion is the reason for the separation of church and state—a principle that aims not at protecting the state from religion but at protecting religion from the state.

To exclude religion is to exclude from politics the deepest moral convictions of millions of citizens.

In the First Amendment, religious freedom is of a piece with, indeed is in the very same sentence with, free speech, free press, free assembly, and the right to challenge government policy. Hence the resolution put before this house flatly contradicts the guarantees of a free and democratic society enshrined in the Constitution of the United States.

Secondly, I urge you to oppose the resolution because it is foolish to attempt to do what by definition cannot be done. Such an attempt can only intensify confusions and conflicts, further polarizing our public life. To exclude religion is to exclude from politics the deepest moral convictions of millions of citizens—indeed, in this society, the great majority of citizens. Thus the resolution before this house is a formula for the death of democracy and should be resolutely defeated.

What do we mean by politics? I believe the best brief answer is proposed by [Greek philosopher] Aristotle. Aristotle teaches that politics is free persons deliberating the question "How ought we to order our life together?" The *ought* in that definition indicates that politics is in its very nature, if not always in its practice, a *moral* enterprise. The very vocabulary of political debate is inescapably moral: What is just? What is unjust? What is fair? What is unfair? What serves the common good? On these questions we all have convictions, and they are moral convictions.

It is not true that our society is divided between a moral majority of the religious, on the one hand, and an immoral or amoral minority of the nonreligious, on the other. Atheists can have moral convictions that are every bit as strong as the moral convictions of the devout Christian or observant Jew. What we have in the political arena is not a division between the moral and the immoral but an ongoing contention between different moral visions addressing *the* political question—how ought we to order our life together?

Our political system calls for an open-ended argument about all the great issues that touch upon the question "How ought *we to order our life together?"*

Democracy in Action

This ongoing contention, this experience of being locked in civil argument, is nothing less than democracy in action. It is [Abraham] Lincoln and [Stephen A.] Douglas debating the morality of slavery; it is the argument about whether unborn children have rights we are obliged to respect; it is the argument over whether the war in Iraq is just or unjust. And on and on. These are all moral arguments to which people bring their best moral judgment. In short, our political system calls for open-ended argument about all the great issues that touch upon the question "How *ought* we to order our life together?"

The idea that some citizens should be excluded from addressing that question because their arguments are religious, or that others should be excluded because their arguments are nonreligious or antireligious, is an idea deeply alien to the representative democracy that this constitutional order is designed to protect. A foundational principle of that order is that all citizens have equal standing in the public square.

But what about the institutions of religion such as churches or synagogues? They may understand themselves to be divinely constituted, but, in the view of the Constitution, they are voluntary associations of citizens who join together for freely chosen purposes. They are in this respect on the same constitutional footing as labor unions, political action groups, professional associations, and a host of other organizations formed by common purpose. In the heat of the political fray, all these institutions are tempted to claim that, on the issues that matter most to them, they have a monopoly on morality. All of them are wrong about that.

Religion cannot be separated from democratic *politics.*

Religious institutions are also—some might say especially—tempted to claim a monopoly on morality. Whether it is the religious right or the much less discussed religious left, their leaders sometimes make a political assertion and then claim, "Thus saith the Lord." Jim Wallis, a prominent leader of the religious left and of the Democratic party's effort to reach so-called values voters, has even written a book with the title *God's Politics*. In his book, he lays out, among many other things, how the prophet Isaiah would rewrite the federal budget of the United States. This is presumption and foolishness of a high order. But the constitutional guarantee of the free exercise of religion guarantees that foolish things will be done in the name of religion. Just as the guarantee of free speech ensures that foolish things will be said in innumerable other causes. We all—left and right, liberal and conservative—have a constitutional right to be stupid.

Religion and Democracy Are Intertwined

As I have suggested, religion *cannot* be separated from politics. More precisely, religion cannot be separated from *democratic* politics. But I do believe that religious leaders should be more circumspect and restrained than they sometimes are in addressing political issues, and that for two reasons. The first and most important reason is that the dynamics of political battle tend to corrupt religion, blurring the distinctions between the temporal and the eternal, the sacred and the profane. So the first concern is for the integrity of religion.

The second concern is for the integrity of politics. Making distinctively religious arguments in political debates tends to be both ineffective and unnecessarily polarizing. Citizens who are religious, like all citizens, should as much as possible make arguments on the basis of public reasons that are accessible to everyone. That is my advice to both the religious left and the religious right, to both Jim Wallis and [televangelist] Pat Robertson. But they are under no constitutional obligation to accept my advice, and, based on past history, they probably won't. Remember the constitutional right to do dumb things.

There is a long and complicated history by which the West, and America in particular, has arrived at our commitment to freedom of religion, freedom of the press, freedom of speech, and freedom of political action. These freedoms, as they are enshrined in the First Amendment, are all of a piece. Our history and our commitment is not shared by everyone in the world. In most dramatic contrast today are Islamic societies in which, as many see it, the brutal choice is posed between monolithic religion or monolithic secularism. We have to hope that is not the case, but that is a problem for Muslims to resolve.

A Pluralistic Society

Thank God, and thank the American Founders, our circumstance is very different. Ours is a pluralistic society in which, by the means of representative democracy, *all* citizens—whether religious, nonreligious, antireligious, or undecided—are on an equal footing as they bring their diverse and sometimes conflicting moral visions to bear on the great question of politics—how *ought* we to order our life together?

The resolution before the house is "Religion and politics should always be kept separate." Because it violates the First Amendment guarantee of the free exercise of religion and associated guarantees such as free speech, because it is alien to the American experience, and because it could not be implemented without undermining the equality essential to a pluralistic and democratic society, I urge you to defeat this profoundly illiberal resolution.

2

Religion and Politics Are Not Separate in America

Paul Jenkins

Paul Jenkins studied international relations and political science in Switzerland, while working as a journalist at news agency AFP (Agence France Presse). He currently is working in the art business.

Politics and religion have meshed so much, that politicians cannot keep their beliefs private. To garner votes of various religious voting blocs, political candidates and elected officials have to embrace religion, regardless of leanings and convictions. Hypocrisy and an uneasy marriage of state and church are the result.

Barack Obama's church-related quandary[1] is just the latest example of American politicians' perilous dance with religion. In a presidential campaign infused like never before with the candidates' efforts to sell their religious beliefs as best-fitting an illusory mainstream, Obama hasn't quite pulled it off, although he is in a far better position after his historic speech in Philadelphia [in March 2008].

Obama's experience should provide another strong indictment of the perverted use of religion in American politics, but the focus has been much narrower, trained on this one pastor and this one church. This is a great shame, although it's hard

1. During the 2008 presidential election, Obama was criticized for attending a church in Chicago that was presided over by Jeremiah Wright, a pastor who made controversial statements during his sermons.

Paul Jenkins, "America's Twisted Marriage of Religion and Politics," *The Huffington Post*, 2008. Copyright © 2008 HuffingtonPost.com. Reproduced by permission.

to deny that Obama should have seen this coming. It's also hard not to fault Obama's need for a religious advisory committee advising his campaign, and for providing a political role to Wright (most of the other campaigns, including [Hillary] Clinton's have gone the same route.) What is wrong with just going to church and not talking about it? Or just not going to church?

Obama is hardly alone in his embrace of the unseemly mix of politics and spirituality.

Obama is hardly alone in his embrace of the unseemly mix of politics and spirituality. Religion as a political marketing tool is nothing new, but this year's campaign is notable if only because the three remaining candidates were not previously known for being happy Christian warriors (as opposed to, say, George W. Bush).

Embracing Religion for Votes

In Obama's case, his initial clumsiness notwithstanding, it is clearly the addition of race to an already combustible mix that his detractors have cunningly latched on. How else can one explain that [2008 Republican candidate] John McCain's recent endorsement by a virulently anti-Catholic televangelist has gone basically unchallenged, with the GOP [Republican party] candidate unmoved by calls to rebuke John Hagee [pastor and founder of John Hagee Ministries]. Hopefully, this comfortable bigotry exhibited by the Episcopalian McCain won't play too well in, say, New Jersey, Pennsylvania and Ohio in November (then again, with Obama having been tarred by the Clinton campaign as a hater of Geraldine Ferraro [former vice presidential candidate] and by extension of all older white Catholic women, Catholic voters in those states may have a tough time picking this fall).

Yet there are worse religious extremists in the GOP than McCain, probably half of the Republican members of congress and governors, including presidential runner-up Mike Huckabee, whose campaign was centered on a breathtakingly stupid literal interpretation of the Bible. This didn't stop the supposedly secular media from a lengthy infatuation with the former Baptist preacher. Essentially ignored were Huckabee's hateful views on a range of issues, from the quarantine of people with AIDS as recently as the 1990s, to equating abortion with slavery. Much more was made of Huckabee's new-style Christianity calling for compassion for "the weak." That is until until "the weak," undocumented immigrants for instance, got between Huckabee and a suddenly attainable White House. Huckabee did apologize, though, for calling Mormonism a devil cult, but of course the harm was done to the Mormon in the race, [Republican candidate] Mitt Romney.

The Anglo-Saxon religious hypocrisy that pervades American politics allows for the most dreadful private behavior, as long as the candidate, when caught, is suitably contrite, seeks "spiritual guidance" and goes to church. A lot.

Romney himself tried to pull the old "as long as we all believe in one God, it's all good" routine, much in vogue with politicians of minority religious beliefs (Joe Lieberman [senator from Connecticut who ran in the 2004 presidential election] came up with his own version in 2000, tempered by upsettingly self-deprecating humor meant to demystify his Orthodox Judaism to vaguely anti-Semitic voters). But Christian conservatives never quite warmed up to Romney and his Mormonism, dooming his candidacy. It's not unfathomable that a number of voters in 2000 rejected Lieberman's Judaism.

Bigotry Abounds

The Anglo-Saxon religious hypocrisy that pervades American politics allows for the most dreadful private behavior, as long as the candidate, when caught, is suitably contrite, seeks "spiritual guidance" and goes to church. A lot.

This is how we ended up in this campaign with a group of holier-than-thou Republican presidential candidates married a total of nine times among the top five (including one-timers Romney and Huckabee). A religious highlight of the campaign was Pat Robertson's endorsement of thrice-married born-again Catholic Rudy Giuliani, he who conducted a lengthy affair with his current wife while still married to Donna Hanover, the mother of his children, who learned of his planned divorce live on local TV.

This is also how we witness a former president, Bill Clinton, in an open marriage to a possible future president, with his wife's increasingly publicized Methodist faith seemingly not interfering much with their marital arrangement. No one has clutched a bible tighter and ambled into a church with as much purpose as Bill did in the aftermath of the Monica Lewinsky disaster. From his Baptist religion's perspective, of course, he compounded his awful sin of adultery with a lie; his wife, we think, only lied about it, but that is also a sin in her Methodist faith. What saved the day for the Clintons, though, in addition to their reinvigorated Christian zeal, is that Bill signed the Defense of Marriage Act which bans the Federal government from recognizing same-sex marriage, right around the time of the Lewinsky and other Clinton sex scandals. This shameful act was surely seen by the Clintons as indispensable to the public defense of their own marriage (and the White House) and is just one of the many betrayals of the couple's core supporters (why their current backers don't see this is a mystery, and a story for another day).

Including Clinton, nearly all the other candidates in this year's presidential race have opposed same-sex marriage, mostly based on their religious beliefs, as [Democratic candidate] John Edwards made clear. In general, gay sex remains far more taboo than its straight version: Bill Clinton got away (gets away?) with sleeping with female interns and assorted subalterns, but Rep. Mark Foley [R-Fla.] was hunted out of Washington for trying to sleep with male pages. Unless they're [former New York Governor] Eliot Spitzer (felled by his own version of the Crusades), male politicians can also comfortably get away with sex with female prostitutes: John Vitter, a lunatic Bible-thumping Senator from Louisiana remains in office to this day, not least because of his appropriately Christian response to being caught (multiple mentions of God and forgiveness; little detail about the actual act to be forgiven). Ethics and laws don't matter much in American government if you can make a religious enough statement of contrition.

The Democratic Party, fearful as always, has gone along with the merging of politics and religion, not wanting to be branded the party of the atheists.

Hiding Behind Religious Statements

For 25 years, many in the Republican Party have hoped to install a theocratic government and have succeeded in incremental ways, with [George W.] Bush as their most recent standard-bearer. The Democratic Party, fearful as always, has gone along with the merging of politics and religion, not wanting to be branded the party of the atheists (in the same way half the Democratic Senators, including Clinton, voted for the Iraq war so they wouldn't be called the party of the pacifists). One recent and sad example of Democrats' attempt at blunting such accusations is the religious caucus in the upcoming [2008] Denver convention. This, however, is sure to backfire, as the party is basically saying that you can't be Latino and/or African-American and/or religious: all three caucuses are held at the same time (as are others.) Maybe it's just that the Democratic National Committee wants to avoid fiery sermons by Jeremiah Wright-style black preachers.

That the United States is a religious country in which 62% believe in the devil, far more than believe in evolution, is one thing. But why drag out religion at every political opportunity, when no ostensibly spiritual politician lives remotely in accordance with his or her publicly stated beliefs? In fact, it's a pretty sure bet that, as they have for centuries, the more public figures exhibit religious fervor, the more likely it is that they are living a lie in their personal life. It may be naive to ask for a little (Christian?) humility, privacy and, more importantly, tolerance, including for the non-religious among us. But it is not more naive than to think that once in a while the unstable fusion of politics and religion won't explode in one or another politician's face.

3

Religion Has Become a Liability in Politics

Johnny No One

Johnny No One is the creation of Bryan Lee Peterson, and he is the voice of the blog and podcast I Hope You're Happy.

Religion was a major factor in the 2008 Presidential election, and the candidates and their fates were closely tied to what religious group or church they embraced. The defeat of Mitt Romney and the difficulties of John McCain and Barack Obama show that displaying one's religion—while expected by voters— has become a liability. It is no longer sufficient to embrace Christianity (all other religions have long been liabilities), but it seems more and more necessary to choose the "right" church. This, however, leads to alienation of others, and forces the candidates to perform a balancing act, that more than once has resulted in awkward and damaging situations. America might have reached the point where religious beliefs must become again a private, not a public, matter for political candidates.

Religion was very interesting in this [2008] election cycle, and it gets more interesting every campaign year. [Democratic candidate Barack] Obama had Reverend [Jeremiah] Wright, [Republican candidate John] McCain had ultra-conservatives that were intolerant bastards. [Republican candidate] Mitt Romney had the unquantifiable Mormon thing. All of this was an issue because their religion wasn't acceptable to a voter demographic. The candidate wasn't one of "them,"

Bryan Lee Peterson, "The Religious Liability," *Johnny No One: I Hope You're Happy*, 2009. Copyright © 2009 I Hope You're Happy. Reproduced by permission.

whoever the "them" happened to be. And don't even try to get into politics if you're an atheist. You obviously have no morals. So here's my topic, and it is an open debate. Is religion becoming such a polarizing force that it is now a liability? Would it be better to not disclose your beliefs and let voters decide based on track record alone whether you uphold their principles?

Religion has always been important to the American voter.

Let's look at some basic points of history. Religion has always been important to the American voter. No way around that. In the past, we were also much more conservative than we are now. And yet, the religious backgrounds of our previous presidents have been varied within the Christian spectrum. I think Jefferson was atheist or agnostic, but that was also back in a period of high public acceptance of atheism. The anti-atheist movement hadn't kicked in yet, though there were certainly similarly conservative forces at work. The smear campaigns were also much more bitter, directed at the morals of a candidate. But at the same time, having a Christian affiliation essentially qualified a person for being, well, Christian. There were some reservations between the sects, but at the national level, some brand of Christianity was good enough for most people.

Now things are different. Christians are divided on what the right brand of Christianity is, and the most vocal at the moment, the conservative sects, are very intolerant of any interpretation of the divine that isn't their own.

So here's the question: how much is faith now dividing voters, and how much is it now a liability to a candidate?

Finding the Right Christian Brand

Let's start by looking at Mitt Romney. He's a very savvy politician, one who could have run a campaign very similar to

Obama's in its new media exploitation, on-line fundraising and business-like focus on issues rather than typical political attacks. When you look at his policy platform, he looks great for conservative voters. He is pro-life, pro family, and pro just about anything that conservative Christians are, while being anti gay marriage and anti just about everything that conservative Christians are. He is also very favorable to big business in a conservative free market kind of way. So what killed his chances for office?

I'm going to say that his campaign was run competently, so that didn't kill his chances. His religion alienated him from core voters who didn't trust anybody who wasn't their brand of Christian. Romney did a huge campaign to market Mormonism as just a variety of Christianity, that he believes in Jesus Christ, and that he wasn't different from all the rest out there whose vote he so sorely needed if he was going to win the nomination. It didn't work.

The Mormons have an image problem beyond their alien beliefs, namely their secrecy and their polygamist past (and present).

Maybe those people didn't trust the vast left wing media in its coverage, or maybe they only listened to their preachers and Fox News saying that he isn't one of them. Mormonism is a sect and world unto itself. In its history, it has been pushed to the fringe of Christianity, run out of Missouri by militias, and forced to make do around the Great Salt Lake, hardly an easy place to settle. This was done by Christians who didn't like an upstart cult that was strange and talked of aliens and things (think Roswell but in a 19th century kind of way). I'd be interested to see how much the early cult talked about Jesus versus how much they try to convince the world of their Christianity now.

The Mormons have an image problem beyond their alien beliefs, namely their secrecy and their polygamist past (and present). Ask for a tour of the Vatican, and you can stop in anytime no matter what your religion. Ask for a tour of The Tabernacle, and they'll close the doors and call the cops. You can't get in unless you're one of the blessed, at least not to the main rooms where worship is done. This led to a suspicion that Romney couldn't possibly overcome the Christian voter's doubts, even though the core of his policies were in line.

Faith Can Be a Liability

Then we get [Vice-Presidential candidate] Sarah Palin. Her faith forced her into some awkward positions on the campaign trail. . . . To go back over this briefly, he [the African pastor who visted Palin's church in Alaska] prayed that she would be freed from witchcraft, and she was criticized for going along with this prayer. In her defense, put in context, witchcraft is a widely held folk belief in Africa. People are still killed for being witches, and mass hysteria similar to what we saw in the Salem witch trials still makes the news coming out of Africa. For him, this is a legitimate prayer according to his belief, and I expressed my hope for Sarah Palin that she regarded it as a backwards folk belief. Then it was pointed out that she believes in fossil fuels, but not in fossils. [Comedian and political commentator] Bill Maher mentioned that she is part of a sect that wants to bring about the kingdom of heaven on Earth (end of the world), and that's a scary thought coming from someone that is a heartbeat away from the button. When [Palin's teenage daughter] Bristol got pregnant, she was confronted with the reality of preaching abstinence to a teenager, and the real fault I find is that she clung to that belief instead of reconsidering the position.

She never had any problems with the conservative Christian base of the Republican party. The problems she ran into was with the moderate voters who wanted to see leadership and innovative thinking, and only saw the same dogmatic leadership of the [George W.] Bush debacle. The movement away from Bush is what allowed McCain to get the nomination. He was viewed as the center-right position that the party leadership says actually represents America. Palin pulled that meter far from the center, and that's what buried him on Nov. 4th.

If you're not bound to a belief system, you can look at an issue and if your solution doesn't work, throw it out and try something else.

The problem is that a dogmatic approach to the world may work for you and your own belief system, but that belief system isn't shared with every person in the world. The solution that seems obvious to a dogma doesn't apply to everyone, and this is why religion and politics shouldn't mix. If you're not bound to a belief system, you can look at an issue and if your solution doesn't work, throw it out and try something else. In Palin's case, she was unbending in her policies despite her failures at home, and that proved that her religion had blinded her from being able to learn from objective data, like that little bump in her unwed teenage daughter's tummy.

Battleground Faith

But let's move on. Elizabeth Dole [former Senator from North Carolina] accused her opponent of being Godless, which is very unbecoming of a southern belle like her. Who taught her etiquette? This attack was designed to divide her opponent from religious voters, but the challenge was to make it stick. Her Democratic opponent Kay Hagan ran a counter ad, smiling, talking of her church experience, and the tactic wound up backfiring, costing Dole the election. Dole lost credibility because of the tone and incredulity of her comments. This was good evidence of both the old tricks not working, and the public tiring of religion being an issue that serves to discredit a candidate.

McCain is not a very religious man. Let's face it. He's somebody that I suspect of being Christian for the sake of his voter demographic. He was endorsed by various religious leaders, but declined a couple as media became vocal about these leaders. One was Rev. John Hagee, who was anti-gay, but also anti-catholic, having called the Catholic Church "the great whore" and "a false cult system." Apparently in a sermon, Hagee said that bible verses made it clear that Hitler and the Holocaust were part of God's plan to chase Jews from Europe and into Palestine. Either this is hating Jews or wishing for the apocalypse. I'm not sure which. . . .

McCain also had problems with James Dobson and Focus on the Family [a conservative, faith-based advocacy group]. I think that in the end, as the crazy came out and the campaign looked more and more desperate, Evangelicals voted for McCain, though probably not in the same numbers they voted for Bush, but throughout the campaign, the Evangelical vote, so important to Republican success, was a big question for McCain. It would be very interesting to know how much these endorsements would have helped McCain, and how much they hurt him in his rejection.

Faith as a Political Weapon

On the Democratic side, Obama suffered attacks by his Democratic rivals about [his pastor] Jeremiah Wright, and those attacks continued from Republicans, though not John McCain, who was smart enough to see them as a side tent to the circus (if only he'd had that foresight about Palin). The Wright thing was overblown so much in the primaries that it was a dead issue by the time the Republicans had the opportunity to exploit it, should they have chosen to do so, and they held off on it until they were down and desperate.

When I looked at those arguments in context, I didn't see a problem with them. Put in the scope of the time and neighborhood and career, they seemed far tamer than even Martin Luther King's sermons at times. It's just the people who aren't used to hearing these kinds of sermons who are having issues with them. They refused to ask the questions of what was the audience of the church, and could we find any events that happened close to the sermons to trigger the fiery rhetoric. Was there a local hate crime, a local KKK [Ku Klux Klan] rally? Maybe an event that made national news? Without looking at these factors, a few lines from a few sermons seem unconnected from any reality that could be used to properly critique them.

As a tangential issue, did you notice the blatantly offensive and false attacks on Obama focused more on his religion than his race. Seems that discrimination against race is more taboo than discrimination based on religion. Ann "C-word" Coulter [a conservative political commentator] based the last two years of her life claiming Obama is Muslim, saying to this day that he will be sworn in on a copy of the Koran. C-word also only refers to Obama as "B. Hussein" to accentuate fear and suspicion in Republican whackadoos who aren't able to think for themselves.

Now, as inauguration looms, Barack Obama has chosen Rick Warren, a pastor who believes that homosexuality can be cured, to deliver a prayer.

Gay Rights and Religion

Let's not forget about Prop[osition] 8. California, who had approved gay marriage voted it down based upon millions of dollars in anti-Prop 8 funding from out of state Mormons and other conservative groups. You may have read my article on the Prop 8 vote, and ironically, this is having a strong influence in dealing with polygamy among fundamentalist Mormon sects. When you look at the argument against gay marriage, it always falls back to a religious point of view, always starts off with "God says . . ." or "The Bible defines . . ." I can't say I've ever heard an argument against gay marriage that doesn't hinge on the good book. Once again, religion is the dividing line on a political issue.

Now, as inauguration looms, Barack Obama has chosen Rick Warren, a pastor who believes that homosexuality can be cured, to deliver a prayer. Having been forcibly dissociated with his religious leader during the campaign, he has been left without the time to find a new spiritual leader, Obama has taken the opportunity to reach out to conservatives with this pick. The choice is inclusive, but it has brought a bitter discussion to the inauguration from the homosexual community, who feel betrayed in it. Eventually Obama selected openly gay Episcopal Bishop Gene Robinson to give a kick-off prayer.

What about an atheist? The Secular Coalition recently surveyed political leaders to find out who was the highest ranking official who would publicly declare himself or herself to be an atheist. They wound up finding California Rep. Pete Stark. When I heard about it, they talked to some of his constituents, who remarked that it didn't seem to make a difference in how he represented them, and that he had done a good job of it.

Atheists Seem to Be Excluded from Higher Office

What if an atheist candidate came out with a strictly by the book Conservative Christian platform, wants to ban abortion, gay marriage, sex ed, the teaching of evolution, all of it. Would that person be embraced by the community for their platform, or would that person be ostracized simply because of a lack of faith in a higher being?

If Mitt Romney had kept his Mormon faith somehow hidden, and I know this is a purely hypothetical, could he have won the Republican primaries? His views were more in line with the base than McCain's, his campaign was well-funded and efficient. He had the charisma. To me all signs point to yes. There was just that question of faith that got in his way.

There's this theme that keeps coming up that is very significant here. It used to be that Christians of various branches could respect one another, but that seems to have changed. Now you have to be the right kind of Christian, if you use the wrong kind of bible, or relax in one fundamental philosophy or another, you are branded a heretic, untrustworthy, and obviously don't have any morals, and have fallen to the devil, given the mark of Cain and all of the usual rigmarole [complex and ritualistic procedure].

I don't want to draw any undo comparisons, but there is something very familiar between an Islamist saying you are all infidels worshipping a false God, and a Republican saying you aren't like us, you're UnAmerican.

I think this is an interesting turning point in politics. The polarization of dialog surrounding religion in politics has caused religion to be a liability, and something that can't be gotten around. I think if a politician somehow kept his religion in the closet, would it be an issue, or would we be more focused on the issues and the platforms of the candidates? At this point in time, that's entirely possible.

Besides, I kind of like the irony of people of faith being forced into the closet.

4

The Role of Religion in Politics Has Grown

Kevin Coe and David Domke

Kevin Coe is a doctoral candidate in speech communication at the University of Illinois. David Domke is professor of communication and head of journalism at the University of Washington. They are authors of the book, The God Strategy: How Religion Became a Political Weapon in America *(Oxford).*

Ever since Ronald Reagan accepted the Republican nomination for president in 1980 and led the audience in a silent prayer, religion has wound its way into the political discourse. Only fifty years ago, the common belief was that views on religion were private, but the past twenty-nine years have seen a steep rise in religiosity, making it more and more difficult for political candidates to avoid statements concerning their church and affiliation.

The 2008 presidential campaign is striking in that it seems to be nearly as much about religion as politics.

[Republican candidate] Mitt Romney's much-discussed speech on faith and politics is just one recent example of a trend that has stretched throughout the campaign and across both sides of the partisan aisle. During the seemingly endless string of debates, candidates have pondered what Jesus would do about capital punishment, raised their hands to deny evolution, considered whether America is a Christian nation, described the power of prayer, and eagerly affirmed that yes, the Bible is indeed the word of God.

Kevin Coe and David Domke, "Think Religion Plays a Bigger Role in Politics Today? You're Right. Statistics Prove It," *History News Network*, 2008. Reproduced by permission.

There was a time when such overt religious displays from presidential hopefuls might have been surprising. Now they're a mundane feature of every serious campaign. How did we get here? In a sense, it all began on July 17, 1980.

Reagan Changed the Political Landscape

That evening, in Detroit's Joe Louis Arena, Ronald Reagan accepted the Republican nomination for president. Fundamentalists and conservative evangelicals, newly mobilized through organizations such as the Moral Majority, had found their man.

For the previous four years this constituency had tried to like Jimmy Carter who, after all, was an openly "born again" Christian. But Carter had disappointed the political faithful with his insufficiently aggressive foreign policy, support for *Roe v. Wade* [the 1973 Supreme Court decision which legalized abortion], and general unwillingness to make his faith demonstrably public. Indeed, Carter in his nomination acceptance addresses in 1976 and 1980 made no mention of God whatsoever.

Reagan had a very different strategy. Approaching the end of his 1980 acceptance speech, Reagan departed from his prepared remarks: "I have thought of something that is not part of my speech and I'm worried over whether I should do it." He paused, then continued:

"Can we doubt that only a Divine Providence placed this land, this island of freedom, here as a refuge for all those people in the world who yearn to breathe freely: Jews and Christians enduring persecution behind the Iron Curtain, the boat people of Southeast Asia, of Cuba and Haiti, the victims of drought and famine in Africa, the freedom fighters of Afghanistan and our own countrymen held in savage captivity."

Reagan went on, "I'll confess that"—and here his voice faltered momentarily—"I've been a little afraid to suggest what I'm going to suggest." A long pause ensued, followed by this:

"I'm more afraid not to. Can we begin our crusade joined to-gether in a moment of silent prayer?" The entire hall went si-lent, heads bowed. He then concluded with words uncommon at the time: "God bless America."

Religion Takes Center Stage

How do we know that this moment marked a turning point? We ran the numbers.

Our analysis of thousands of public communications across eight decades shows that American politics today is de-fined by a calculated, demonstrably public religiosity unlike anything in modern history. Consider a few examples.

Presidential requests for divine favor also show a pro-found shift.

If one looks at nearly 360 major speeches that presidents from Franklin Roosevelt [FDR] to George W. Bush have given, the increase in religiosity is astounding. The average president from FDR to Carter mentioned God in a minority of his speeches, doing so about 47% of the time. Reagan, in contrast, mentioned God in 96% of his speeches. George H. W. Bush did so 91% of the time, Clinton 93%, and the current [George W.] Bush (through year six) was at 94%. Further, the total number of references to God in the average presidential speech since 1981 is 120% higher than the average speech from 1933–1980. References to broader religious terms, such as faith, pray, sacred, worship, crusade, and dozens of others increased by 60%.

Presidential requests for divine favor also show a profound shift. The phrase "God Bless America," now the signature tagline of American politics, gained ubiquity in the 1980s. Prior to 1981, the phrase had only once passed a modern president's lips in a major address: Richard Nixon's, as he con-cluded an April 30, 1973, speech about the Watergate scandal.

Since Reagan, presidents have rarely concluded a major address without "God Bless America" or a close variant.

Politicians Are Courting People of Faith

Recent presidents have also made far more "pilgrimages" to speak to audiences of faith. From FDR through Carter, presidents averaged 5.3 public remarks before overtly religious organizations in a four-year term. Beginning with Reagan through six years of Bush, this average more than tripled to 16.6 per term. For example, since 1981 GOP [Republican] presidents have spoken 13 times to the National Association of Evangelicals or the National Religious Broadcasters Association, four times to the Knights of Columbus, and four times to the Southern Baptist Convention. Clinton never spoke to these conservative organizations; instead, he spoke in churches. From FDR through Carter, presidents delivered public remarks in churches an average of twice per four-year term. In contrast, Clinton spoke in churches 28 times during two terms in the White House—10 more visits than Reagan, Bush Sr. and Bush Jr. combined.

Wherever we looked, whatever we measure, we find the same pattern. Presidents and presidential hopefuls since Reagan have been afraid to be seen as the apostate [someone who criticizes or renounces his or her former religion] in the room. They put religion front and center to show they're not.

This new age is one that many past presidents would hardly recognize. One can't help but wonder what would become of a candidate today who, like John Kennedy in 1960, "believe[s] in a president whose views on religion are his own private affair."

5

Black Evangelicals Have Become a Social and Political Force

Krissah Williams

Krissah Williams is a Washington Post *staff writer.*

Although many African American voters traditionally support Democratic candidates, the Republican party (GOP) is eager to change that. Trying to convince evangelical African Americans to join their cause, their focus has been on social issues such as gay rights and abortion. Even though black voters might be socially conservative, they are politically progressive, and both Democrats and Republicans are aware of the growing importance of that voting bloc. Yet many African American pastors are disappointed with the GOP and with Democrats alike, because they believe previous administrations have not followed up on election promises.

Pastor Harry R. Jackson Jr. will often exhort his congregation to "stand against" abortion and same-sex marriage. "You are on the battlefield in a culture war," he'll say, urging his listeners to help serve as the "moral compass of America."

In his rhetoric and his political agenda, Jackson has much in common with other evangelical Christians who are part of the conservative wing of the Republican party [GOP], except that Jackson is African American and so is his congregation at Hope Christian Church in Prince George's County [Maryland].

Jackson, head of a group of socially conservative black pastors called the High Impact Leadership Coalition, in many ways personifies the possibilities that Republican strategists such as Karl Rove have seen in appealing to the social conservatism of many African American churchgoers. Blacks overwhelmingly identify themselves as Democrats and typically support Democratic candidates, but optimists in the GOP think one way to become a majority party is to peel off a sizable segment of black voters by finding common ground on social issues.

As a group, blacks attend religious services more frequently than whites and are less supportive of gay rights.

Differing Views on Social Issues

As a group, blacks attend religious services more frequently than whites and are less supportive of gay rights. In a *Washington Post*-Kaiser Family Foundation-Harvard University poll this summer [2007], 43 percent of white Democrats supported same-sex marriage, about double the percentage of black Democrats who said they do. More than half of blacks said they oppose both same-sex marriage and legal recognition of same-sex civil unions.

In the 2004 election, there was evidence that an appeal aimed at those differences could work. President [George W.] Bush nearly doubled his share of the black vote in Ohio, thanks to a same-sex-marriage initiative on the ballot and the targeting of black churchgoers through mailings and radio ads. But it's unlikely that the 2008 Republican presidential candidate will be able to consolidate those gains, and Jackson is one indication of why.

During the last presidential election cycle, Jackson prayed for Bush and crisscrossed the country pressing conservative social issues. Now he's pushing an issues agenda rather than "carrying the water for the Republican party," he said. "They are not reliable enough."

Jackson's discontent is a reflection of the worries of other religious conservatives, black and white, who fear that Republican voters will nominate pro-choice candidate and former New York mayor Rudolph W. Giuliani and are still chafing at the headline-grabbing sex and ethics scandals involving Republicans.

Republicans Lack Appeal

"You don't have someone who is a Christian evangelical like [George W.] Bush to really revitalize the black evangelicals this time around," said John C. Green, senior fellow at the Pew Forum on Religion and Public Life. Bush promised colorblind appointments and launched the faith-based initiative, and the timing of his run coincided with several state ballot initiatives banning same-sex marriage that turned out large numbers of evangelicals, Green said. The Republicans running this year have not made the same appeal.

Other conservative black preachers raise a different issue.

"Morality is different in terms of the way we see it and white evangelicals see it," said Pastor Lyle Dukes of Harvest Life Changers Church in Woodbridge [Virginia], a member of Jackson's group who supported Bush in 2004. "What we think is moral is not only the defense of marriage, but we also think equal education is a moral issue. We think discrimination is immoral."

Dukes is looking at candidates in both parties this year.

Bishop Timothy J. Clarke, leader of the 5,000-member First Church of God in Columbus, Ohio, said: "You have to prioritize. You are dealing with a less-than-perfect world and a less-than-perfect system."

Clarke has worked with Jackson's coalition but also hosted Democratic presidential candidates in 2004. He said he and his members care as much about health care and livable wages as they do about conservative social issues.

Relevance Trumps Dogma for Many

On his way out of the noon Bible study at Metropolitan African Methodist Episcopal Church in the District [Washington, D.C.] the other day, Stephen Peagler, 27, said he is a faithful churchgoer who believes that abortion and same-sex marriage are wrong. But, he said, when it comes to voting, he's looking for a candidate who will address issues that are more relevant in his everyday life. And Democrats are more likely to deal with the high incarceration rates of black men and underperforming inner-city schools, he said.

And there is a more fundamental obstacle that anyone seeking a vote for GOP candidates must confront: "I was brought up to say that the Republicans are not good, and they are not for issues that concern blacks," Peagler said.

The black evangelical church developed a penchant for social justice and progressive politics as part of the civil rights movement of the 1960s.

Only 5 percent of blacks in the latest *Washington Post-ABC News* poll called abortion or moral or family-values issues their top concerns for the upcoming presidential election. By contrast, more than four in 10 highlighted the war in Iraq, 38 percent health care and 33 percent the economy and jobs.

"Devout black churchgoers' issue set is pretty much the same as other African Americans, which is big on economic issues, health care and dealing with poverty and education," said David Bositis of the Joint Center for Political and Economic Studies. "When African Americans say they are conservative, it doesn't mean they are politically conservative. It means that they are conservative in terms of their personal behavior."

Different Takes on Conservatism

The evangelical church's racial split turns on that point. The black evangelical church developed a penchant for social justice and progressive politics as part of the civil rights movement of the 1960s. White fundamentalists steered clear and after the passage of *Roe v. Wade* made fighting legalized abortion their signature political issue.

"One of the misnomers that we labor under is the line of demarcation between social issues and moral issues," Clarke said. "For us, they are almost one and the same."

Jackson tells both black and white evangelical groups that they have to shake off the past and realize that they now have more in common than they think. At a recent gathering of white evangelical voters in Washington, he described "a new generation of African American preachers who are preaching this same cornbread-and-beans encouraging message, but they have a laptop and BlackBerry. They are informed. They share your values."

Republican officials, for their part, have not given up their efforts to reach church members.

That line elicited a standing ovation from the white crowd, who welcomed the black minister with the same shouts that later greeted Republican presidential candidate and former Arkansas governor Mike Huckabee and conservative Christian leader James Dobson.

Republican officials, for their part, have not given up their efforts to reach church members. The Republican National Committee [RNC] sent representatives to the recent National Baptist Convention in Philadelphia, the National Progressive

Baptist Convention in the District, and the 100th anniversary celebration of the Church of God in Christ in Memphis [Tennessee] to interact with black pastors, according to Shannon Reeves, who oversees the RNC's efforts to increase its following among blacks.

"What they preach from the pulpit is consistent with [Republican] policies, but there was not an organized effort to have an ongoing relationship," Reeves said. "This is long-term."

Republicans Might Be Losing Ground

But Jackson, at least, has become more skeptical about the party.

He thinks the GOP pays attention to evangelicals when it needs their votes but has not delivered when it comes to advancing their causes. Jackson said that after the 2004 election, he attended a White House meeting of evangelical leaders and listened as Rove said he didn't think the church vote had won the election for Bush.

Jackson told him: "I am a registered Democrat. The only reason I am here is because I thought you were working on issues of faith and that it would be better for my folks than the promises, promises of the Democratic party."

Democrats, he said, "come to us under the cloak of darkness at the last hour, get what they want and then act like they don't know us the next day."

That got a big laugh from the conservatives, he recalled. Then Jackson said he told Rove: "You all are doing the same thing to the evangelicals."

6

Christian Fundamentalists Threaten American Freedom

Rob Boston

Rob Boston is the assistant director of communications for Americans United for Separation of Church and State.

Ever since the 1970s, the Religious Right has expanded its influence in the political sphere, and now influences or controls many decisions within the Republican Party. Indeed, candidates for higher office need the blessing of Evangelicals to mount a successful campaign. The Religious Right seeks to control every major social issue, from limiting sex education, to banning gay marriage, to changing school curricula and public education. It seeks to redefine modern society according to a narrow interpretation of the Bible.

Focus on the Family [a conservative faith-based advocacy group] founder James C. Dobson flew into Washington, D.C., last month [May 2006] with twin goals: attend a meeting of the secretive Council for National Policy and issue a new round of orders to top Republican leaders.

With November elections fast approaching, Dobson is eager to make sure the Republican leadership does all it can to satisfy social conservatives. What GOP [Republican party] leaders in Congress have done so far—subjecting Supreme Court appointments to a right-wing litmus test, steadily eroding legal abortion, allocating billions in tax money to religious groups, curbing comprehensive sex education in public institutions, intervening in personal end-of-life decisions in the Terri Schiavo case and laboring to make same-sex marriage unconstitutional—is apparently not enough. Dobson has more items on his wish list.

In a series of meetings with top Republican leaders, Dobson made it clear that he expects action now. Otherwise, as he remarked on Fox News Channel's "Hannity & Colmes" May 1, "I think there's going to be some trouble down the road if they don't get on the ball."

Republicans Listen to the Christian Right

The Republican leadership, facing an increasingly unfavorable political outlook, moved quickly to placate Dobson. *The New York Times* reported that he met with a list of GOP leaders, among them Karl Rove, top aide to President George W. Bush; U.S. Sen. Bill Frist, Senate majority leader; Speaker of the House Dennis Hastert and U.S. Rep. John A. Boehner, House majority leader.

Religious Right organizations brag about what they hope to achieve on their Web sites and in their publications.

This is the extent of Dobson's power: Religious conservatives enjoy great influence over the federal courts, and their social agenda is being implemented item by item. But it is never enough. Dobson growls, and the top leaders of American politics rush to assure him that all is well. The incident is also a good example of the influence the Religious Right holds in the Republican Party, and thus the larger political system, today.

As Dobson's outburst makes clear, Religious Right groups have a specific set of goals for American life. They speak openly of "taking back" America, of asserting control over the lives of every single citizen. They have an agenda, and they want action on it.

None of this is a secret. Religious Right organizations brag about what they hope to achieve on their Web sites and in their publications. They hold national meetings and conventions to plot strategy. Their leaders issue marching orders to millions of American followers over radio, television and the Internet.

Yet many Americans remain unaware of the scope of the power, money and aspirations of the Religious Right—or how radical its goals are. More than 25 years have passed since a band of conservative strategists convinced the Rev. Jerry Falwell to lead the Moral Majority, and the movement is today at the apex of its political power.

The reign of [George W.] Bush, the first president truly wedded to the Religious Right's agenda, has focused new attention on the movement. . . .

Americans United [AU] has monitored the Religious Right since the movement's genesis with the rise of Falwell in 1979. *AU* staffers read Religious Right publications and monitor group Web sites, radio and television broadcasts as well as other media. *AU* staff members also frequently attend Religious Right gatherings to get an insider's view of the movement. This approach gives *AU* a unique perspective that few outsiders can match.

There Is No "War on Christians"

The information *AU* has compiled provides a compelling counterpoint to claims of a "war on Christians" in American society. According to *AU's* analysis, the nation's top ten Religious Right groups are hardly persecuted. They raked in nearly half a billion dollars collectively. (Some organizational budget figures are from 2004, and some are from 2005. The collective total is $447,368,625.) These groups are well organized, well funded and have specific policy goals.

Republican leaders in Washington are so obsessed with keeping the Religious Right happy that they have established a "Values Action Team" in the House headed by U.S. Rep. Joseph Pitts (R-Pa.) and a Senate version headed by U.S. Sen. Sam Brownback (R-Kan.). The units serve as special liaisons between Congress and the Religious Right. Far from being relegated to the back of the public policy bus, Religious Right lobbyists are often sitting in the driver's seat.

The Religious Right has grown so powerful it enjoys a veto over many national Republican candidates.

The Religious Right has grown so powerful it enjoys a veto over many national Republican candidates. Any Republican who aspires to the presidency must first get a blessing from the Religious Right. A 2002 survey by researchers John C. Green of the University of Akron and Kimberly H. Conger, then a graduate student at Ohio State University, found that the Religious Right has a strong position in 18 state GOP affiliates and a moderate position in 26. In only seven states was its influence described as weak.

This phenomenon played out most recently with U.S. Sen. John McCain's well-publicized apology to Falwell.

Appeasing the Christian Right

In [the presidential election campaign of] 2000, McCain lashed out at Falwell and others in the Religious Right, calling them "agents of intolerance." McCain, gearing up for another run in 2008, recently met with Falwell privately in his Senate office, where the two mended fences.

"He put his hand out and said, 'I said those words. I was emotional. It was the heat of the moment. I'm sorry,'" Falwell told *Congressional Quarterly*. "I said, 'No apology necessary, senator. Let's move on.'" McCain also agreed to give the commencement address at Falwell's Liberty University.

Many Religious Right figures hold leadership positions in the GOP. For example, "Christian nation" advocate David Barton is vice-chairman of the Texas Republican Party. Former Christian Coalition head Ralph Reed is currently running for lieutenant governor in Georgia. Gary Bauer, who headed the Family Research Council for 10 years, sought the Republican presidential nomination in 2000.

Political scholar and former Republican strategist Kevin Phillips, writing in an April 2 [2006] opinion piece in *The Washington Post*, was blunt: "Now that the GOP has been transformed by the rise of the South, the trauma of terrorism and George W. Bush's conviction that God wanted him to be president, a deeper conclusion can be drawn: The Republican Party has become the first religious party in U.S. history."

Religious Right groups also enjoy great access to the public through the media. Much religious broadcasting also promotes far-right politics. These television and radio broadcasts are omnipresent. In October [2005], Knight-Ridder Newspapers reported, "The growth in the number of religious stations has been marked: Of 13,838 radio stations in the United States, 2,014 are religious stations, according to Arbitron Inc., the media research company. That's up from 1,089 stations among 12,840 in 1998, according to Arbitron. Salem Communications Corp., of Camarillo, Calif., the biggest owner of Christian stations, owns 104 radio stations in the country and syndicates programming to 1,900 affiliates."

The story singled out several Christian TV networks as well, among them Pat Robertson's Christian Broadcasting Network, Trinity Broadcasting, Inspiration Network, Daystar, Three Angels Broadcasting, World Harvest Television, Cornerstone Television, Praise TV, Worship Channel, Gospel Music Television, The Word Network and FamilyNet.

Religious Programming Is on the Rise

"If you wanted to, you could immerse yourself 24 hours a day in religious programming in nearly every radio market in the country or with cable television or with satellite TV," said Quentin J. Schultze, author of *Televangelism in America: The Business of Popular Religion* and a professor of communications at Calvin College, in Grand Rapids, Mich.

Mainline Christianity, which consists of more politically moderate Protestant denominations, has nothing that matches the reach of conservative Christianity over the airwaves.

Religious Right groups also have a considerable strategizing and planning network in place that magnifies their influence. Despite some competition among groups for funding and members, movement leaders are savvy enough to see the value in coalition work. The Council for National Policy (CNP), for example, is an umbrella organization that brings Religious Right leaders together for regular "war council" meetings where strategy is plotted, information is shared and candidates are vetted. ([George W.] Bush met with the CNP prior to the 2000 election. To this day, no one knows what he told the group.)

On paper, the Fairfax, Va.-based CNP does not look like much. Public documents show that its annual budget is less than $1 million. It has a tiny staff, and, due to its secretive nature, rarely makes headlines.

Mainline Christianity, which consists of more politically moderate Protestant denominations, has nothing that matches the reach of conservative Christianity over the airwaves.

But the CNP's influence has been profound, and it has real clout. Last month, the group met at the Ritz-Carlton Hotel in Tysons Corner, Va., to celebrate its 25th anniversary. Scheduled speakers included U.S. Sen. George Allen (R-Va.), widely acknowledged as a leading contender for the Republican presidential nomination in 2008; U.S. Sen. Rick Santorum (R-Pa.); Department of Homeland Security Secretary Michael Chertoff and U.S. Ambassador to the United Nations John Bolton.

Despite this ability to bring in right-wing heavy hitters, few Americans have heard of the CNP. ABC News, in fact, has called the CNP "the most powerful conservative group you've never heard of."

Another umbrella organization, the Arlington Group, is named for the D.C. suburb in Virginia where it meets to plot new ways to oppose gay rights. Founded by leaders from 10 Religious Right organizations in 2002, the Arlington Group now includes more than 50 members. Paul Weyrich of the Free Congress Research and Education Foundation boasted in 2005 that the coalition has had a dramatic impact on politics.

"For the first time, virtually all of the social issues groups are singing off the same sheet of music," said Weyrich. "This has never happened before. From the beginning of the pro-life movement through the development of the pro-family movement, everybody did their own thing. But working together we have helped to re-elect the president and added a number of conservative senators." . . .

What the Religious Right Wants

Advocates of separation of church and state are often accused of being shrill or alarmist when they assert that Religious Right groups favor theocratic government. But an honest look at the facts leaves any other conclusion hard to draw. Modern Religious Right groups might not press overtly for writing their understanding of Christianity into the Constitution, but their agenda, if implemented, would force Americans to live under a system of laws based on fundamentalist interpretations of the Bible.

Religious Right leaders frequently speak of their mandate to take "dominion" over American society or impose a "biblical worldview." An entire Religious Right organization, Worldview Weekend, exists to train activists in ways to impose their version of faith on all aspects of society, including government.

To the Religious Right, the Bible mandates that fundamentalist Christians assert control over society at all levels.

As TV preacher D. James Kennedy put it in his 1997 book *Character & Destiny*, "This is our land. This is our world. This is our heritage, and with God's help, we shall reclaim this nation for Jesus Christ. And no power on earth can stop us."

To the Religious Right, the Bible mandates that fundamentalist Christians assert control over society at all levels. This viewpoint leads some extremists to embrace what can only be called spiritual totalitarianism.

A document issued by the Coalition on Revival, a group aligned with Christian Reconstructionism, stated bluntly, "We deny that anyone, Jew or Gentile, believer or unbeliever, private person or public official, is exempt from the moral and juridical obligation before God to submit to Christ's Lordship over every aspect of his life in thought, word and deed."

Controlling Americans' Decisions About Reproduction, Sex, and Death

Religious Right groups seek to interfere in the most intimate areas of our lives. Most oppose legal abortion for any reason. They advocate "abstinence-based" sex education programs in public schools and other forums, even though most experts agree this approach is ineffective, inaccurate and even dangerous because it does not discuss condoms and artificial forms of birth control.

The Religious Right's influence here has been considerable. A recent poll cited by *The New York Times Magazine* noted that more than 90 percent of Americans favor comprehensive sex education in public institutions that includes topics like birth control. Yet millions of dollars in federal funds pay for so-called "abstinence education," which by law excludes contraceptive information. The same article noted the increase in opposition to artificial forms of contraception by fundamentalist Protestants. Yielding to this pressure, the Food and Drug Administration under Bush has refused to approve "morning after" pills that are routinely used in Europe.[1]. . .

Religious Right groups support the so-called "right" of pharmacists to refuse to dispense birth control and other medications, and they even seek the right to determine how we will die. In the famous case of Terri Schiavo in Florida, a phalanx of Religious Right organizations prodded Gov. Jeb Bush, the U.S. Congress and President Bush to intervene in a personal family matter in an effort to keep a woman in a persistent vegetative state alive against her stated wishes.

Stem-cell research, which holds the promise of finding cures for debilitating sicknesses like Parkinson's Disease and Alzheimer's Disease, has been consistently hampered by the Bush administration, thanks to Religious Right demands.

Passing Anti-Gay Laws

Attacks on gay people are a standard Religious Right ploy. According to Religious Right leaders, gays are sinners who must be converted to fundamentalist Christianity (and thus heterosexuality). Attempts to end discrimination on the basis of sexual orientation amount to "special rights." They oppose not only same-sex marriage but in many states have lobbied

1. The morning after pill was approved by the FDA in 2006 for women ages eighteen and over without a prescription. In 2009, over the counter access was extended to seventeen-year-old women as well.

for other restrictions on gays, such as striking down local domestic partnership laws and barring gays from adopting or becoming foster parents.

Gay-related controversies are a perfect wedge issue for the Religious Right. The groups have exploited them skillfully, spearheading drives to add anti-same-sex marriage provisions to 19 state constitutions. They also seek to do the same to the federal Constitution.

Religious Right groups have a long track record of activism in this area, and the rhetoric they employ is often shrill. In 1994, a collection of 40 Religious Right groups met at a retreat in Colorado to plot strategy. At the meeting, a staffer with Focus on the Family remarked, "I think the gay agenda—and I would not say this as frankly as I will now in other cultural contexts—I think the gay agenda has all the elements of that which is truly evil. It is deceptive at every turn. . . . It is destroying the souls and the lives of those who embrace it, and it has a corrosive effect on the society which endorses it, either explicitly or even implicitly."

Religious Right leaders favor a system of home schools or fundamentalist academies backed by taxpayer subsidies.

Controlling Education in America

The Religious Right has alternated for years between wanting to seize total control of public education or advocating shutting it down entirely. To the Religious Right, education not infused with fundamentalist dogma is useless and an affront to God.

In a 1979 book, Falwell observed, "One day, I hope in the next ten years, I trust that we will have more Christian day schools than there are public schools. I hope I will live to see the day when, as in the early days of our country, we won't have any public schools. The churches will have taken them over again and Christians will be running them. What a happy day that will be!"

Although Falwell is embarrassed by the quote today and tries to shrug it off, it remains a good summary of the Religious Right's goals for public education. Books bashing public schools are a staple among the Religious Right. In recent years, the Southern Baptist Convention, which is controlled by fundamentalists, has considered resolutions calling on church members to withdraw their children from public schools. Religious Right leaders favor a system of home schools or fundamentalist academies backed by taxpayer subsidies. They may be well on their way to getting it. The Supreme Court upheld vouchers in 2002.

In the meantime, Religious Right groups work to "Christianize" public education—and the Christianity they want is of the fundamentalist variety. Some push for the reintroduction of Bible study and coercive forms of school prayer. Others attack the teaching of evolution or want inaccurate "Christian nation" views of American history taught.

Aware that 90 percent of American children attend public schools, Religious Right organizations use various methods of subterfuge to proselytize this "captive audience."

While Americans United and its allies have been successful in fending off many schemes to infuse public education with sectarian dogma, new battles continue apace. Disputes over evolution are a good example. Church-state separation advocates have won every major court battle in this arena, but the controversy generated over the issue has made textbook publishers skittish. As a result, many public schools give scant attention to evolution, even though it is considered the lynchpin of the biological sciences.

7

Pastors Should Be Allowed to Endorse Candidates in Sermons

Erik Stanley

Erik Stanley is senior legal counsel and head of the Alliance Defense Fund's Pulpit Initiative.

It has been argued that pastors cannot endorse political candidates during sermons, because this would violate the churches' tax-exempt status. But the Internal Revenue Service (IRS) should not try to restrict pastors' free speech rights. Taxing churches is a way to destroy religion and undermines the First Amendment. Pastors do not have to talk about politics, but should be free to do so.

Every election season, the debate over faith in public life is sure to take center stage. It should.

The debate embodies the intersection of two of America's most cherished freedoms: free speech and religious liberty. Americans long have believed that, in a free society, such debate should continue—inside and outside the church—without government interference. That's why we have the First Amendment, and that's why the Alliance Defense Fund has mounted a challenge to a portion of the federal tax code that violates it. The alliance's Pulpit Initiative will culminate Sunday [September 28, 2008] in a sermon delivered by several dozen pastors nationwide who will evaluate candidates for elective offices and how their positions line up with Scripture. The plan to free pastors from unconstitutional restrictions has been met with misguided opposition, and that includes a press conference last week in Columbus.

Arguing that a tax agency should hold veto power over sermon content is like arguing that the Department of Transportation should decide a school lunch menu.

Legal Issues Surrounding Church Practices

Leading it was the Rev. Eric Williams of the North Congregational United Church of Christ [Columbus, Ohio], a pastor whom the alliance invited to participate in the initiative, and whose denomination the alliance offered to assist when the IRS [Internal Revenue Service] investigated (and subsequently and rightly cleared) it for politicking. Williams protested the very project that would help protect him and his church. And he's called for the IRS to investigate the alliance.

Yes, that's ironic. But most who oppose the initiative misunderstand it. Others, however, understand it too well and *prefer* the climate of fear under which pastors operate.

The Pulpit Initiative is not about serving any candidate or political party; it is about restoring the right of pastors to speak freely from the pulpit without fear of punishment by the government for doing what churches do: speak on any number of cultural and societal issues from a biblical perspective. That includes commenting on the positions of political candidates, if they so choose. The initiative is not a demand that churches discuss candidate positions. The point is that it's up to the church to decide, according to the Constitution and the exercise of religious faith.

Arguing that a tax agency should hold veto power over sermon content is like arguing that the Department of Transportation should decide a school lunch menu. Pastors spoke freely about the policy positions of candidates for elective office throughout American history, even endorsing or opposing candidates from the pulpit, without anyone ever questioning whether churches should remain tax exempt. It was common, indeed expected, for pastors to speak in support of or in opposition to candidates until the Johnson Amendment [which prohibits nonprofit organizations, including churches, from endorsing or opposing political candidates] was inserted quietly into the tax code in 1954, with no legislative analysis or debate.

The state cannot demand the surrender of constitutional rights for a church to remain tax exempt.

Free Speech Includes Pastors

Most scholars recognize that the amendment had nothing to do with churches. It was cleverly designed to silence some nonprofit organizations who opposed Lyndon B. Johnson's Senate campaign in Texas. But that hasn't stopped activist groups from wielding the IRS weapon to silence churches across the country. The tax agency's rule is unconstitutional because it muzzles free speech and improperly entangles the state in church affairs.

The state cannot demand the surrender of constitutional rights for a church to remain tax exempt.

Nonprofit organizations are exempted because they are not profit-makers. If citizens are already taxed on their individual incomes, taxing their participation in a voluntary organization from which they derive no monetary gain amounts to double taxation.

Churches are all the more tax exempt. Church tax-exemption is not a gift or a subsidy, as some disingenuously contend. As the U.S. Supreme Court has noted, the power to tax involves the power to destroy, and churches always have been exempt from taxation under the principle that there is no surer way to destroy religion than to tax it.

The Separation of State and Church

And how ironic is it that those who wave the banner of separation of church and state are the loudest voices demanding that the government entangle itself in the most intimate church business, namely the content of pastors' sermons? Americans United for Separation of Church and State, the group that has made its name using the tax man as an ax man, recently wrote, "Constitutional violations do not get grandfathered in simply because of the passage of time."

The organization should listen to its own words. The Johnson Amendment is an ax that's been around for a half century, but that doesn't make it constitutional. It is surefire to destroy the free exercise of religion. It's time to get the government out of the pulpit.

8

Pastors Should Not Be Allowed to Endorse Candidates in Sermons

Barry W. Lynn

Reverend Barry W. Lynn has been the executive director of Americans United for Separation of Church and State since 1992. He is an ordained minister in the United Church of Christ.

As nonprofit organizations, churches are rightly restricted from becoming "political machines." Far from restricting a pastor's right to voice his personal opinions, this keeps elections fair and democratic. Religious leaders can advocate social change, but they should not use their tax-exempt status to endorse candidates from the pulpit.

Most Americans who go to church expect to hear about salvation, morality, and scripture. They don't anticipate hardball political endorsements.

Congress made it clear in 1954 that nonprofit groups, religious or secular, may not endorse or oppose any candidate for public office.

That doesn't mean pastors, priests, rabbis, or imams cannot criticize government policies. It doesn't mean clergy cannot express views on specific pieces of legislation or ballot initiatives. Nor does it even mean they cannot participate in partisan political activities in their own personal capacity.

What it does signify is that pastors cannot make declarations to favor or oppose any candidate from the pulpit. They cannot take money from the collection plate and give it to support a candidate. And if they want to participate in any partisan activity in their personal capacity, they must make sure it is done in a manner indicating it is separate from their religious institution.

Put simply, the tax code prevents religious institutions from serving as political machines, a concept in keeping with the separation of church and state our founding fathers envisioned.

Churches Should Not Act as Political Machines

Put simply, the tax code prevents religious institutions from serving as political machines, a concept in keeping with the separation of church and state our founding fathers envisioned.

Now a group called the Alliance Defense Fund is working to alter that vision. The group recently urged pastors around the country to violate tax law and promote candidates from the pulpit. Thirty-three pastors participated. But we all know churches in America are already free to engage in religious speech. Tax law doesn't take that freedom away.

We know this because the Revs. Jerry Falwell (on the right) and William Sloane Coffin (on the left) weren't silenced from speaking from the pulpit on moral issues. And the regulation never prohibited the Rev. Martin Luther King Jr. from speaking passionately of the need for social change in our country—while never once endorsing a candidate from the pulpit.

It's clear that the law as it is provides those of us in the clergy with an astounding amount of freedom to express a wide array of opinions from the pulpit. But we cannot turn sermons into political ads for candidates, nor should we have that "freedom." In a recent survey on this issue, 87 percent of Americans agreed that pastors shouldn't endorse candidates during worship services. Americans clearly see that churches should not become cogs in anybody's political machine.

Politics Take a Toll on Congregations

Americans also recognize politics can split congregations.

Take, for example, the church in Waynesville, N.C., where the Rev. Chan Chandler told congregants during a sermon in October 2004, "If you vote for John Kerry this year, you need to repent or resign." This comment tore apart the congregation, initially leading to the ouster of nine Democratic members. Following a congregational meeting, they were invited back to the church and Chandler was forced to resign.

If a church doesn't want to follow IRS law, it can refuse the tax exemption.

More recently at High Point Church in Arlington, Texas, Pastor Gary Simons showed a video that depicted the views of Barack Obama and John McCain on abortion. His sermon gave God's alleged view on abortion and told the congregation how to vote accordingly. Some congregants said the pastor seemed to be comparing Obama to King Herod, the biblical monarch who ordered the mass murder of infants. Several members just walked out.

Frankly, a tax exemption is a privilege, not a right. The IRS [Internal Revenue Service] can strip a church of its tax exemption for egregious violations of law. It did just that to the Church at Pierce Creek in Binghamton, N.Y. In 1992, the church spent $44,000 on an ad in *USA Today* that called Bill Clinton a sinner and warned Christians against voting for him. The congregation contested the revocation in court but lost at every level. Not one judge agreed the church had some sort of "free speech" or "free exercise" right to engage in partisan activities

This is not a First Amendment concern but a ploy for groups like the Alliance Defense Fund to use churches to push a political agenda. If a church doesn't want to follow IRS law, it can refuse the tax exemption. But churches that want this privilege have to play by the same rules as everyone else.

9

Religion's Role in Gay Marriage Violates Separation of Church and State

Geoffrey Stone

Geoffrey Stone is the Edward H. Levi Distinguished Service Professor of Law at the University of Chicago. He is the author of Perilous Times: Free Speech in Wartime, from the Sedition Act of 1798 to the War on Terrorism.

In a democracy, the majority decides political issues, but it should not restrict basic human rights and disenfranchise minorities. California's Proposition 8, which sought to ban same-sex marriage, is an attempt to suppress personal rights and force religious beliefs and codes of behavior on everyone, including nonbelievers. Narrow-minded interpretations of faith often have led to self-righteousness and oppression of others, and they are again on the rise.

How can a free society reconcile the often competing values of democracy, religious liberty and the separation of church and state? This challenge was vividly illustrated by the recent [2008] controversy over California's Proposition 8, which forbade same-sex marriage.

In a democracy, the majority of citizens ordinarily may enact whatever laws they want. Some laws, however, are prohibited by the Constitution. For example, the majority of citizens may want a law denying African-Americans the right to vote or prohibiting Muslims from attending public schools, but such laws violate the Constitution.

Does Proposition 8 violate the Constitution? There are several arguments one might make for this position. One might argue that Proposition 8 discriminates against gays and lesbians in violation of the Equal Protection Clause. One might argue that Proposition 8 unconstitutionally limits the fundamental right to marry. One might argue that Proposition 8 violates the separation of church and state. It is this last argument that interests me.

The Separation of State and Church

Laws that violate the separation of church and state usually take one of two forms. Either they discriminate against certain religions ("Jews may not serve as jurors"), or they endorse particular religions ("school children must recite the Lord's Prayer"). Proposition 8 does not violate the principle of separation of church and state in either of these ways. It neither restricts religious freedom nor endorses religious expression.

What it does do, however, is to enact into law a particular religious belief. Indeed, despite invocations of tradition, morality and family values, it seems clear that the only honest explanation for Proposition 8 is religion. This is obvious not only from the extraordinary efforts undertaken by some religious groups to promote Proposition 8, but also from the very striking voting patterns revealed in the exit polls.

Proposition 8 was enacted by a vote of 52% to 48%. Those identifying themselves as Evangelicals, however, supported Proposition 8 by a margin of 81% to 19%, and those who say they attend church services weekly supported Proposition 8 by a vote of 84% to 16%. Non-Christians, by the way, opposed Proposition 8 by a margin 85% to 15% and those who do not attend church regularly opposed Proposition 8 by a vote of 83% to 17%.

What this tells us, quite strikingly, is that Proposition 8 was a highly successful effort of a particular religious group to conscript the power of the state to impose their religious beliefs on their fellow citizens, whether or not those citizens share those beliefs. This is a serious threat to a free society committed to the principle of separation of church and state.

The Framers of the American Constitution knew that throughout human history religious self-righteousness has caused intolerance, discrimination and injustice.

A Serious Threat to Democracy

The Framers of the American Constitution knew that throughout human history religious self-righteousness has caused intolerance, discrimination and injustice. They understood that religious self-righteousness is dangerous, divisive and destructive, and that it has led to untold ignorance and misery. It was for that reason that they embedded in our Constitution a fundamental commitment to the separation of church and state.

The Framers were not anti-religion. They understood that religion could help to nurture the public morality necessary to a self-governing society. But religion was to be fundamentally private. It was for the individual. It was not to intrude unduly into the political sphere.

But here's the rub: From a strictly legal perspective, it is next to impossible for courts to enforce the separation of church and state in the context of laws like Proposition 8. When a law does not directly restrict religious activity or expressly endorse religious expression, it is exceedingly difficult for courts to sort out the "real" motivations behind the law. As a consequence, courts are loath to invalidate laws on the ground that they enact a particular religious faith.

This does not end the inquiry, however. Courts also have difficulty in dealing with laws that do not expressly discriminate on the basis of race or religion or gender, but that were motivated by racial, religious or gender prejudice. But we know—as an essential part of our national character—that we as citizens should not support laws because they advance our discriminatory biases about race, religion, and gender. We know that it is un-American for us to enact laws because they implement our prejudices. We know that it is our responsibility to be tolerant, self-critical and introspective about our own values and beliefs and to strive to achieve our highest national aspirations.

The fundamental point about religious liberty in the United States is that it is private.

The Abuse of the Power of the State

The separation of church and state is one of those aspirations. Indeed, regardless of whether courts can intervene in this context, it is as un-American to violate the separation of church and state by using the power of the state to impose our religious beliefs on others as it is to use the power of the state to impose our discriminatory views of race, religion or gender on others.

This is the fundamental point that the religious advocates of Proposition 8 fail to comprehend. Like other citizens, they are free in our society to support laws because they believe those laws serve legitimate ends, including such values as tradition, general conceptions of morality, and family stability. But they are not free—not if they are to act as faithful American citizens—to impose their religious views on others. That is, quite simply, un-American.

This is not to say that individuals cannot attempt to persuade others freely to embrace and to act in accord with their religious beliefs. The First Amendment gives us virtually absolute protection to preach, proselytize and evangelize. But the fundamental point about religious liberty in the United States is that it is private. Christian Evangelicals have every right to try to persuade others to accept and abide by their beliefs. But they have no right—indeed, they violate the very spirit of the American Constitution—when they attempt to conscript the authority of the state to compel those who do not share their religious beliefs to act as if they do.

10

Religion Is Influencing Global Politics

Timothy Samuel Shah and Monica Duffy Toft

Timothy Samuel Shah is a senior fellow in religion and world affairs at the Pew Forum on Religion and Public Life. Monica Duffy Toft is associate professor of public policy at Harvard's Kennedy School of Government and director of the Initiative on Religion on International Affairs. She is the author of The Geography of Ethnic Violence *and* Securing the Peace.

Although at one time the spread of democracy seemed to put religion on the sidelines, it has made a comeback in recent decades. Religiosity is on the rise in developed as well as underdeveloped nations. The new movements have shed archaic connotations and are tech-savvy and most often conservative. Modernization and globalization, which were once thought to bring about more secular times, have largely strengthened politicized religion instead.

Religion was supposed to fade away as globalization and freedom spread. Instead, it's booming around the world, often deciding who gets elected. And the divine intervention is just beginning. Democracy is giving people a voice, and more and more, they want to talk about God.

After Hamas [a Palestinian Islamic organization that includes a paramilitary force] won a decisive victory in January's

[2006] Palestinian elections, one of its supporters replaced the national flag that flew over parliament with its emerald-green banner heralding, "There is no God but God, and Muhammad is His Prophet."

Days after the prophet's banner was unfurled in Ramallah, thousands of Muslims mounted a vigorous, sometimes violent, defense of the prophet's honor in cities as far-flung as Beirut [Lebanon], Jakarta [Indonesia], London [United Kingdom] and New Delhi [India]. Outraged by cartoons of Muhammad originally published in Denmark [September 2005], Islamic groups, governments and individuals staged demonstrations, boycotts and embassy attacks.

On their own, these events appeared to be sudden eruptions of "Muslim rage." In fact, they were only the most recent outbreaks of a deep undercurrent that has been gathering force for decades and extends far beyond the Muslim world.

Whether the field of battle is democratic elections or the more inchoate struggle for global public opinion, religious groups are increasingly competitive.

Prophetic Politics

Global politics is increasingly marked by what could be called "prophetic politics." Voices claiming transcendent authority are filling public spaces and winning key political contests. These movements come in very different forms and employ widely varying tools. But whether the field of battle is democratic elections or the more inchoate struggle for global public opinion, religious groups are increasingly competitive. In contest after contest, when people are given a choice between the sacred and the secular, faith prevails.

God is on a winning streak. It was reflected in the 1979 Iranian revolution, the rise of the Taliban in Afghanistan, the Shia revival and religious strife in postwar Iraq, and Hamas's recent victory in Palestine and Israel's struggle with Hezbollah in Lebanon. But not all the thunderbolts have been hurled by Allah.

The struggle against apartheid in South Africa in the 1980s and early 1990s was strengthened by prominent Christian leaders such as Archbishop Desmond K. Tutu. Hindu nationalists in India stunned the international community when they unseated India's ruling party in 1998 and then tested nuclear weapons.

American evangelicals continue to surprise the U.S. foreign-policy establishment with their activism and influence on issues such as religious freedom, sex trafficking, Sudan and AIDS in Africa. Indeed, evangelicals have emerged as such a powerful force that religion was a stronger predictor of vote choice in the 2004 U.S. presidential election than was gender, age, or class.

The spread of democracy, far from checking the power of militant religious activists, will probably only enhance the reach of prophetic political movements, many of which will emerge from democratic processes more organized, more popular, and more legitimate than before—but quite possibly no less violent.

The Rise and Fall of Secularism

It did not always seem this way. In April 1966, *Time* ran a cover story that asked, "Is God Dead?" It was a fair question. Secularism dominated world politics in the mid-1960s. The conventional wisdom shared by many intellectual and political elites was that modernization would inevitably extinguish religion's vitality. But if 1966 was the zenith of secularism's self-confidence, the next year marked the beginning of the end of its global hegemony.

In 1967, the leader of secular Arab nationalism, Gamal Abdel Nasser, suffered a humiliating defeat at the hands of the Israeli armed forces. By the end of the 1970s, Iran's Ayatollah

Khomeini, avowedly "born-again" U.S. President Jimmy Carter, television evangelist Jerry Falwell and Pope John Paul II were all walking the world stage.

A decade later, rosary-wielding Solidarity members in Poland and Kalashnikov-toting mujahedeen in Afghanistan helped defeat atheistic Soviet communism. A dozen years later [September 11, 2001], 19 hijackers screaming "God is great" transformed world politics.

Today [August 2006], the secular pan-Arabism of Nasser has given way to the millennarian pan-Islamism of Iranian President Mahmoud Ahmadinejad, whose religious harangues against America and Israel resonate with millions of Muslims, Sunni and Shia alike. "We increasingly see that people around the world are flocking towards a main focal point—that is the Almighty God," Ahmadinejad declared in his recent letter to President [George W.] Bush.

This comes as the world indeed becomes more modern: It enjoys more political freedom, more democracy and more education than perhaps at any time in history.

It is also wealthier. The average share of people in developing countries living on less than a dollar a day fell from 28 percent to 22 percent between 1990 and 2002, according to World Bank estimates.

But this has not led to people becoming more secular. In fact, the period in which economic and political modernization has been most intense—the past 30 to 40 years—has witnessed a jump in religious vitality around the world.

Growing Religious Observance

According to the *World Christian Encyclopedia*, a greater proportion of the world's population adhered to the major religious systems in 2000—Christianity's Catholicism and Protestanism, Islam and Hinduism—than a century earlier.

At the beginning of the 20th century, a bare majority of the world's people, precisely 50 percent, were Catholic, Protestant, Muslim or Hindu. At the beginning of the 21st century, nearly 64 percent were. The proportion may be close to 70 percent by 2025.

Not only is religious observance spreading, it is becoming more devout.

The World Values Survey, which covers 85 percent of the world's population, confirms religion's growing vitality. According to scholars Ronald Inglehart and Pippa Norris, "the world as a whole now has more people with traditional religious views than ever before—and they constitute a growing proportion of the world's population."

Not only is religious observance spreading, it is becoming more devout. In Brazil, China, Nigeria, Russia, South Africa and the United States, religiosity became more vigorous between 1990 and 2001.

Between 1987 and 1997, surveys by the Times Mirror Center and the Pew Research Center registered increases of 10 percent or more in the proportions of Americans surveyed who "strongly agreed" that God existed, that they would have to answer for their sins before God, that God performs miracles, and that prayer was an important part of their daily life. Even in Europe, a secular stronghold, there have been surprising upticks in religiosity.

The Influence of Expanding Freedom

God's comeback is in no small part due to the global expansion of freedom. People in dozens of countries have been empowered to shape their public lives in ways that were inconceivable in the 1950s and 1960s. In country after country, politically empowered groups began to challenge the secular constraints imposed by the first generation of modernizing, post-independence leaders.

Often, as in communist countries, secular straitjackets had been imposed by sheer coercion; in other cases, as in Atatürk's Turkey, Nehru's India, and Nasser's Egypt, secularism retained legitimacy because elites considered it essential to national integration and modernization—and because of the sheer charisma of these countries' founding fathers. In Latin America, right-wing dictatorships, sometimes in cahoots with the Catholic Church, imposed restrictions that severely limited grass-roots religious influences, particularly from "liberation theology" and Protestant "sects."

As politics liberalized in countries like India, Mexico, Nigeria, Turkey, and Indonesia in the late 1990s, religion's influence on political life increased dramatically. Even in the United States, evangelicals exercised a growing influence on the Republican Party in the 1980s and 1990s, partly because the presidential nomination process depended more on popular primaries and less on the decisions of traditional party leaders. Where political systems reflect people's values, they usually reflect people's strong religious beliefs.

Marriage of Religion and Politics

Many observers are quick to dismiss religion's advance into the political sphere as the product of elites manipulating sacred symbols to mobilize the masses. In fact, the marriage of religion with politics is often welcomed, if not demanded, by people around the world.

In a 2002 Pew Global Attitudes survey, 91 percent of Nigerians and 76 percent of Bangladeshis agreed that religious leaders should be more involved in politics. A June 2004 six-nation survey reported that "most Arabs polled said that they wanted the clergy to play a bigger role in politics." In the same survey, majorities or pluralities in Morocco, Saudi Arabia, Jordan and the United Arab Emirates cited Islam as their primary identity, trumping nationality.

The collapse of the quasi-secular Baathist dictatorship in Iraq released religious and ethnic allegiances and has helped Islam play a dominant role in the country's political life, including in its recently adopted constitution. Evangelicals have become an influential voting bloc in numerous Latin American countries, including Brazil, Guatemala, and Nicaragua.

The most dynamic religiosity today is not so much "old-time religion" as it is radical, modern and conservative.

Far from stamping out religion, modernization has spawned a new generation of savvy and technologically adept religious movements, including evangelical Protestantism in America, "Hindutva" in India, Salafist and Wahhabi Islam in the Middle East, Pentecostalism in Africa and Latin America, and Opus Dei and the charismatic movement in the Catholic Church. The most dynamic religiosity today is not so much "old-time religion" as it is radical, modern and conservative.

Modern Religion, Technology, and Politics

A common denominator of these neo-orthodoxies is the deployment of sophisticated and politically capable organizations. These modern organizations effectively marshal specialized institutions as well as the latest technologies to recruit new members, strengthen connections with old ones, deliver social services, and press their agenda in the public sphere.

The Vishwa Hindu Parishad, founded in 1964, "saffronized" [converted] large swaths of India through its religious and social activism and laid the groundwork for the Bharatiya Janata Party's electoral successes in the 1990s. Similar groups in the Islamic world include the Muslim Brotherhood in Egypt and Jordan, Hamas in the Palestinian territories, Hezbollah in Lebanon, and the Nahdlatul Ulama in Indonesia. In Brazil, pentecostals have organized their own legislative caucus, representing 10 percent of congresspeople.

Today's neo-orthodoxies may effectively use the tools of the modern world, but how compatible are they with modern democracy? Religious radicals, after all, can quickly short-circuit democracy by winning power and then excluding non-believers. Just as dangerous, politicized religion can spark civil conflict. Since 2000, 43 percent of civil wars have been religious (only a quarter were religiously inspired in the 1940s and 1950s). Extreme religious ideology is, of course, a leading motivation for most transnational terrorist attacks.

The scorecard isn't all negative, however. Religion has mobilized millions of people to oppose authoritarian regimes, inaugurate democratic transitions, support human rights and relieve human suffering.

Today's religious movements, however, may not have as much success in promoting sustainable freedom. Catholicism's highly centralized and organized character made it an effective competitor with the state, and its institutional tradition helped it adapt to democratic politics. Islam and pentecostalism, by contrast, are not centralized under a single leadership or doctrine that can respond coherently to fast-moving social or political events. Local religious authorities are often tempted to radicalize in order to compensate for their weakness vis-a-vis the state or to challenge more established figures.

The trajectory of the young [radical, Shiite] cleric Moqtada al-Sadr in postwar Iraq is not unusual. The lack of a higher authority for religious elites might explain why most religious civil wars since 1940—34 of 42—have involved Islam, with nine of these being Muslim versus Muslim. We need look no further than Iraq today to see religious authorities successfully challenging the forces of secularism—but also violently competing with each other.

Even in a longstanding democracy like India, the political trajectory of Hindu nationalism has demonstrated that democratic institutions do not necessarily moderate these instincts: Where radical Hindu nationalists have had the right mix of opportunities and incentives, they have used religious violence to win elections, most dramatically in the state of Gujarat.

The belief that outbreaks of politicized religion are temporary detours on the road to secularization was plausible in 1976, 1986, or even 1996. Today, the argument is untenable. As a framework for explaining and predicting the course of global politics, secularism is increasingly unsound. God is winning in global politics. And modernization, democratization, and globalization have only made him stronger.

11

Religion Could Bring About Peace and Justice

Joan Bakewell

Dame Joan Bakewell is an English journalist and radio and television commentator.

Britain's ruling class largely ignores religion as a force to shape policies, yet in Burma (Union of Myanmar), thousands of Buddhist monks make their presence felt as they protest against a restrictive and oppressive regime. While the outside world has imposed sanctions on the country and positions itself to influence Burma's domestic politics, the monks' protests show that change must be supported by the citizens. Religion and faith might be one way to bring about that change.

What place do spiritual values have in shaping and defining the policy of the country? It's a question that would certainly not be asked at a UK [United Kingdom] party conference. Other than an occasional grace said before meals, our institutions pay little heed to the religious lives of their people.

As a secular country, we rarely regard the pronouncements of the established church as applying to us. The monastic orders are in sharp decline, and their empty old buildings are being put to other uses. So it is odd to read of a place where empty monasteries bear eloquent witness to political crisis.

The Religious Influence on a Dictatorship

Burma's monasteries have been emptied by a military dictatorship that fears their influence. Only 10 days ago [September 2007], they were right to do so. The sight of tens of thousands of saffron-robed, shaven-headed monks was curiously awesome. They streamed through the streets of Rangoon, for all the world like the terracotta army come alive. People began to speak of the saffron revolution. Their demeanour told us much about modesty, obedience and shared values.

But what exactly did the Buddhist people of Burma expect to happen? They may have hoped to infiltrate some spiritual unease among individuals in the junta [a group controlling the government]. It's said these men are strongly superstitious, believing in astrology and the influence of magical numbers. Apparently monks can exercise a sort of excommunication that can damage their karma, ruin their afterlife.

But it is a strange kind of politics, and it has not yet effected any positive change. The sheer number of the monks must count for something. Clearly Buddhism, with its message of non-violence and philosophy of contemplation, is active throughout the country. The monks come from the people and are largely from the countryside. Pledged to a life of simplicity and prayer, they are respected by villagers and citizens from whom they daily beg alms. No one seems to question their right to be idle and dependent.

The real change must come from within the country.

Individuals can become monks for a few years of their lives, then revert to the way of life they came from. All this is strange and mystifying to the western mindset. The nearest we come is the religious retreat, a form of quick-fix, spiritual renewal enjoying a modish revival in the west. What is clear to everyone, east and west, is that the monks and the movement they support for democratic government, have a heroic leader sharing their outlook and degree of commitment. Aung San Suu Kyi is the daughter of Burma's independence hero, Aung

San. She has the credentials typical of Asia's ruling dynasties—the Gandhis, the Bhuttos—and that must certainly appeal. But she has much more.

At a time of her life when it should be full of joy and fulfilment, she took it upon herself to give up the familiar ways of the world. The interests of her husband—who died without her at his bedside—and her two growing sons, were to come second. She opted for an alternative that has involved almost permanent house arrest, periods of solitary confinement, the junta's rejection of the democratic party she leads, and the crushing of all those who offer her support. Not even the most devout of monks could be making as great a sacrifice as she is. What she is giving them is inspiration.

The Religious Resources Are Put to the Test

The rest of the world discusses further sanctions, castigates Total oil for its trade with Burma, urges China to exercise its influence. The UN [United Nations] envoy Mr [Ibrahim] Gambari comes and goes. ASEAN, the Association of Southeast Asian Nations, threatens to ratchet up diplomatic pressure. All these moves are the stuff of realpolitik, Church leaders worldwide deplore what is happening, bloggers from both Burma and China call on people to wear Red T-shirts as a show of solidarity, and numerous petitions are circulating on the internet. Worldwide popular reactions spill into a void from which all we now hear is of empty monasteries and rumours of slaughter.

So where will the difference be made? Will Burma's spiritual resources be effective, or simply die away in resignation? We must trust that the impact of the monks' peaceful protests is finally effective. Aung San Suu Kyi's hopes must rest with the 400,000-strong army itself. Many soldiers must number monks among their family and friends. If their Buddhist values have sunk deep enough, then the army itself will split and enough soldiers who take their Buddhism seriously will rebel against their orders and fracture the power of the junta. The real change must come from within the country. It must come from within its unhappy population, and it must come from the strength of individual religious conviction.

If it does, then Buddhism may have something to teach us all. It would not be about the prevailing strength of one religious faction against another, of, as it were, Catholic against Protestant or Sunni against Shia. It would be about the collective power of peace and contemplation to bring about justice. We in the west have never given it a try.

12

Christian Fundamentalists Influence U.S. Policies in the Middle East

Stephen Zunes

Stephen Zunes is an associate professor of politics and chair of the peace and justice studies program at the University of San Francisco. He serves as Middle East editor for the Foreign Policy in Focus *project and is the author of* Tinderbox: U.S. Middle East Policy and the Roots of Terrorism.

By adopting conservative goals on social issues, the Republican party has managed to gain votes from low-income evangelicals, who otherwise had little reason to support it. This mobilization has led to more and more religious leaders influencing everyday politics in America and abroad. In the case of Israel, the Religious Right has embraced an aggressive pro-Israel, anti-Palestinian stance, and Christian right-wing Zionists make their influence felt in Washington. Since religion has changed the culture in Washington to the point where it is impossible for candidates to renounce it, mainstream churches need to make their influence felt, to curb the right-wing fundamentalists' stranglehold on foreign politics.

In recent years a politicized and right-wing Protestant fundamentalist movement has emerged as a major factor in U.S. support for the policies of the rightist Likud [a center-right political party] government in Israel. To understand this influence, it is important to recognize that the rise of the religious right as a political force in the United States is a relatively recent phenomenon that emerged as part of a calculated strategy by leading right-wingers in the Republican Party who—while not fundamentalist Christians themselves—recognized the need to enlist the support of this key segment of the American population in order to achieve political power.

Traditionally, American fundamentalist Protestants were not particularly active in national politics, long seen as worldly and corrupt. This changed in the late 1970s as part of a calculated effort by conservative Republican operatives who recognized that as long as the Republican Party was primarily identified with militaristic foreign policies and economic proposals that favored the wealthy, it would remain a minority party. Over the previous five decades, Republicans had won only four out of 12 presidential elections and had controlled Congress for only two of its 24 sessions.

Those who identify with the religious right are now more likely than the average American to vote and to be politically active.

By mobilizing rightist religious leaders and adopting conservative positions on highly-charged social issues such as women's rights, abortion, sex education, and homosexuality, Republican strategists were able to bring millions of fundamentalist Christians—who as a result of their lower-than-average income were not otherwise inclined to vote Republican—into their party. Through such organizations as the Moral Majority and the Christian Coalition, the GOP [Republican party] promoted a right-wing political agenda through radio and television broadcasts as well as from the pulpit. Since capturing this pivotal constituency, Republicans have won four out of six presidential races, have dominated the

Senate for seven out of 12 sessions, and have controlled the House of Representatives for the past decade.

As a result of being politically wooed, those who identify with the religious right are now more likely than the average American to vote and to be politically active. The Christian Right constitutes nearly one out of seven American voters and determines the agenda of the Republican Party in about half of the states, particularly in the South and Midwest. A top Republican staffer noted: "Christian conservatives have proved to be the political base for most Republicans. Many of these guys, especially the leadership, are real believers in this stuff, and so are their constituents."

The Movement Takes Office

The Rev. Barry Lynn of Americans United for Separation of Church and State recently quipped: "The good news is that the Christian Coalition is fundamentally collapsing. The bad news is that the people who ran it are all in the government." He noted, for example, that when he goes to the Justice Department, he keeps seeing lawyers formerly employed by prominent right-wing fundamentalist preacher Pat Robertson.

American liberals have long supported Israel as a refuge for persecuted Jews and have championed the country's democratic institutions (for its Jewish citizens).

As the *Washington Post* observed, "For the first time since religious conservatives became a modern political movement, the president of the United States has become the movement's de facto leader." Former Christian Coalition leader Ralph Reed marked the triumph by chortling, "You're no longer throwing rocks at the building; you're in the building." He added that God "knew George [W.] Bush had the ability to lead in this compelling way."

American liberals have long supported Israel as a refuge for persecuted Jews and have championed the country's democratic institutions (for its Jewish citizens). Historically these liberals, bolstered by the disproportionate political influence of Zionist Jews within the party, prompted Democrats to adopt a hard line toward Palestinians and other Arabs. Though more hawkish on most foreign policy issues, Republicans traditionally took a somewhat more moderate stance partly due to the party's ties to the oil industry and in part because of GOP concern that too much support for Israel could lead Arab nationalists toward a pro-Soviet or—in more recent years—a pro-Islamist orientation. But this alignment has shifted, thanks to the influence of the Christian Right. Though Christian fundamentalist support for Israel dates back many years, only recently has it become one of the movement's major issues.

American Jews and the Christian Right

As a result of renewed fundamentalist interest in Israel and in recognition of the movement's political influence, American Jews are less reluctant to team up with the Christian Right. Fundamentalist leader Gary Bauer, for example, now receives frequent invitations to address mainstream Jewish organizations, which would have been hesitant toward the movement prior to the Bush presidency. This is partly a phenomenon of demographics: Jews constitute only 3 percent of the U.S. population, and barely half of them support the current Israeli government.

The Israelis also recognize the Christian Right's political clout. Since 2001, Bauer has met with several Israeli Cabinet members and with Prime Minister Ariel Sharon. Former Prime Minister Benyamin Netanyahu noted, "We have no greater friends and allies" than right-wing American Christians.

It used to be that Republican administrations had the ability to withstand pressure from Zionist lobbying groups when it was deemed important for American interests. For example, the [Dwight D.] Eisenhower administration pressured Israel during the Suez Crisis of 1956, the [Ronald] Reagan administration sold [Airborne Warning and Control System] AWACS-equipped planes to Saudi Arabia in 1981, and the first [George H.W.] Bush administration delayed a $10 billion loan guarantee for Israel to await the outcome of the pivotal 1992 Israeli election.

With the growing influence of the Christian Right, however, such detachment is no longer as easily achieved. For the first time, the Republican Party has a significant pro-Israel constituency of its own that it cannot ignore. Top White House officials, including Elliott Abrams, director of the National Security Council on Near East and North African Affairs, have regular and often lengthy meetings with representatives of the Christian Right. As one leading Republican put it: "They are very vocal and have shifted the center of gravity toward Israel and against concessions. It colors the environment in which decisions are being made." Indeed, the degree of the [George W.] Bush administration's support for Prime Minister Sharon has surprised even the most hard-line Zionist Jews.

Rising Power of Christian Zionists

It appears, then, that right-wing Christian Zionists are, at this point, more significant in the formulation of U.S. policy toward Israel than are Jewish Zionists, as illustrated by three recent incidents.

- After the [George W.] Bush administration's initial condemnation of the attempted assassination of militant Palestinian Islamist Abdel Aziz Rantisi in June 2003, the Christian Right mobilized its constituents to send thousands of e-mails to the White House protesting the criticism. A key element in these e-mails was the threat that if such pressure continued to be placed upon Israel, the Christian Right would stay home on Election

Day. Within 24 hours, there was a notable change in tone by the president. Indeed, when Rantisi fell victim to a successful Israeli assassination in April 2004, the administration—as it did with the assassination of Hamas leader Sheik Ahmed Yassin the previous month—largely defended the Israeli action.

- When the Bush administration insisted that Israel stop its April 2002 military offensive in the West Bank, the White House received over 100,000 e-mails from Christian conservatives in protest of its criticism. Almost immediately, President Bush came to Israel's defense. Over the objections of the State Department, the Republican-led Congress adopted resolutions supporting Israel's actions and blaming the violence exclusively on the Palestinians.

- When President Bush announced his support for the Road Map for Middle East Peace, the White House received more than 50,000 postcards over the next two weeks from Christian conservatives opposing any plan that called for the establishment of a Palestinian state. The administration quickly backpedaled, and the once-highly touted Road Map essentially died.

Theological Influences: Good Versus Evil

Messianic theology is centered around the belief in a hegemonic [taking leadership over others] Israel as a necessary precursor to the second coming of Christ. Although this doctrine is certainly an important part of the Christian Right's support of a militaristic and expansionist Jewish state, fundamentalist Christian Zionism in America ascribes to an even more dangerous dogma: that of Manichaeism, the belief that reality is divided into absolute good and absolute evil.

The day after the terrorist attacks of September 11, 2001, President Bush declared, "This will be a monumental struggle of good versus evil, but good will prevail." America was targeted—according to President Bush—not on account of U.S. support for Arab dictatorships, the large U.S. military presence in the Middle East, U.S. backing of the Israeli occupation, or the humanitarian consequences of U.S. policy toward Iraq but simply because they "hate our freedom." Despite the Gospels' insistence that the line separating good and evil does not run between nations but rather within each person, President Bush cited Christological texts to support his war aims in the Middle East, declaring, "And the light [America] has shown in the darkness [the enemies of America], and the darkness will not overcome it [American shall conquer its enemies]."

President Bush believes that he has accepted the responsibility of leading the free world as part of God's plan.

Even more disturbingly, Bush has stated repeatedly that he was "called" by God to run for president. Veteran journalist Bob Woodward noted, "The President was casting his mission and that of the country in the grand vision of God's Master Plan," wherein he promised, in his own words, "to export death and violence to the four corners of the earth in defense of this great country and rid the world of evil." In short, President Bush believes that he has accepted the responsibility of leading the free world as part of God's plan. He even told then-Palestinian Prime Minister Mahmoud Abbas that "God told me to strike al-Qaida and I struck them, and then he instructed me to strike at Saddam, which I did." Iraq has become the new Babylon, and the "war on terrorism" has succeeded the Cold War with the Soviet Union as the quintessential battle between good and evil.

Cultural Affinities

The esprit that many Americans have with Israel is rooted in a common historical mission. Each country was settled in part by victims fleeing religious persecution who fashioned a new nation rooted in high ideals with a political system based upon relatively progressive and democratic institutions. And both peoples established their new nations through the oppression, massacre, and dislocation of indigenous populations. Like many Israelis, Americans often confuse genuine religious faith with nationalist ideology.

John Winthrop, the influential 17th century Puritan theologian, saw America as the "City on the Hill" (Zion) and "a light upon nations." In effect, there is a kind of American Zionism assuming a divinely inspired singularity that excuses what would otherwise be considered unacceptable behavior. Just as Winthrop defended the slaughter of the indigenous Pequot peoples of colonial Massachusetts as part of a divine plan, 19th century theologians defended America's westward expansion as "manifest destiny" and the will of God. Such theologically rooted aggrandizement did not stop at the Pacific Ocean: the invasion of the Philippines in the 1890s was justified by President William McKinley and others as part of an effort to "uplift" and "Christianize" the natives, ignoring the fact that the Filipinos (who by that time had nearly rid the country of Spanish colonialists and had established the first democratic constitution in Asia) were already over 90 percent Christian.

Similarly, today—in the eyes of the Christian Right—the Bush Doctrine and the expansion of American military and economic power is all part of a divine plan. For example, in their 2003 Christmas card, Vice President Dick Cheney and his wife Lynne included the quote, "And if a sparrow cannot fall to the ground without His notice, is it probable that an empire can rise without His aid?"

But is such thinking normative in the United States? Polls show that the ideological gap between Christian conservatives and other Americans regarding the U.S. invasion of Iraq and the "war on terrorism" is even higher than the ideological gap between Christian conservatives and other Americans regarding Israel and Palestine.

In many respects, much of the American right may be at least as concerned about how Israel can help the United States as about how the United States can help Israel. Due to the anti-Semitism inherent in much of Christian Zionist theology, it has long been recognized that U.S. fundamentalist support for Israel does not stem from a concern for the Jewish people per se but rather from a desire to leverage Jewish jingoism to hasten the Second Coming of Christ. Such opportunism is also true of those who—for theological or other reasons—seek to advance the American Empire in the Middle East. And though a strong case can be made that U.S. support for the Israeli occupation ultimately hurts U.S. interests, there remains a widely held perception that Israel is an important asset to American strategic objectives in the Middle East and beyond.

Strategic Calculation Trumps Ethno-Religious Card

Ultimately, Washington's championing of Israel—like its approval of other repressive governments—is part of a strategic calculation rather than simply ethnic politics. When a choice must be made, geopolitical considerations outweigh ethnic loyalties. For example, for nearly a quarter of century, the United States supported the brutal occupation of East Timor by Indonesia and to this day supports the Moroccan occupation of Western Sahara, despite the absence of powerful Indonesian-American or Moroccan-American ethnic lobbying forces. The United States was able to get away with its support for occupations by Indonesia and Morocco due to their relative obscurity. This is certainly not the case with Israel and Palestine. (Interestingly, even though the East Timor situation involved a predominantly Muslim country conquering, occupying, and terrorizing a predominantly Christian country, virtually no protests arose from the Islamaphobic Christian Right.)

The Christian Right has long been a favorite target for the Democratic Party, particularly its liberal wing, since most Americans are profoundly disturbed by fundamentalists of any kind influencing policies of a government with a centuries-old tradition of separating church and state. Yet the positions of most liberal Democrats in Congress regarding the Israeli-Palestinian conflict are far closer to those of the reactionary Christian Coalition than to those of the moderate National Council of Churches, far closer to the rightist Rev. Pat Robertson than to the leftist Rev. William Sloan Coffin, far closer to the ultraconservative Moral Majority than to the liberal Churches for Middle East Peace, and far closer to the fundamentalist Southern Baptist Convention than to any of the mainline Protestant churches. Rather than accusing these erstwhile liberals of being captives of the Jewish lobby—a charge that inevitably leads to the countercharge of anti-Semitism—those who support justice for the Palestinians should instead reproach congressional Democrats for falling captive to the Christian Right. Such a rebuke would be no less accurate and would likely enhance the ability of those who support peace, justice, and the rule of law to highlight the profound immorality of congressional sanction for the Israeli occupation.

Those who support justice for the Palestinians—or even simply the enforcement of basic international humanitarian law—must go beyond raising awareness of the issue to directly confronting those whose acquiescence facilitates current repressive attitudes. It will not be possible to counter the influence of the Christian Right in shaping American policies in the Middle East as long as otherwise-socially conscious Christian legislators and other progressive-minded elected officials are beholden to fundamentalist voting pressures. It is unlikely that these Democrats and moderate Republicans will change, however, until liberal-to-mainline churches mobilize their resources toward demanding justice as strongly as right-wing fundamentalists have mobilized their resources in support of repression.

13

Christian Fundamentalists Influence America's Anti-Muslim Foreign Policy

Yoginder Sikand

Yoginder Sikand is an Indian writer-academic and the editor and primary writer of Qalandar, *a monthly electronic publication covering relations between Muslims and followers of other religions. He is the author of* Sacred Spaces: Exploring Traditions of Shared Faith in India.

Christian fundamentalism has shaped America's foreign policy and pitted it against Muslims all over the world. Having gained influence in Washington, they seek to silence all 'non-believers' and impose their world views in the United States and abroad. Their rhetoric has shaped the conflicts in Afghanistan, Iraq, and Palestine, and has led to the portrayal of Muslims as irrational and radical villains. The influence of the Southern Baptist Convention and like-minded evangelical groups might cause more confrontations in the Middle East and around the world, if it is not challenged by more moderate forces.

Although rarely commented on in the press, Christian fundamentalism has emerged as a powerful factor in shaping American foreign policies, particularly in the 'Muslim world'. With a born-again Christian fundamentalist as President of America [George W. Bush] this is hardly surprising. And that this can only further worsen already embittered relations between the 'West' and the 'Muslim world' is too obvious to need any explanation.

Yoginder Sikand, "Christian Fundamentalists: War for Souls and Empire," *American Muslim Perspective*, 2006. Reproduced by permission.

Right-wing evangelical American Christian groups in America are among the most vociferous [clamorous] supporters of Bush's global 'war on terror'. As they see it, all religions other than (their version of) Christianity are nothing less than inventions of the Devil. Their followers, they insist, are doomed to eternal perdition in hell. For them, America's current 'war on terror' is nothing less than a divine mandate to America to break down the walls of heathendom, paving the way for them to pursue what they call their global commission to spread the 'good news' of Christianity.

Churches Are Backing Invasions

The Southern Baptist Convention (SBC) is one of the several American evangelical groups strongly backing Bush's imperialist offensives in Iraq and elsewhere in the 'Muslim world'. Established in 1845, the SBC is the largest and most powerful ultra-conservative Protestant Christian organisation in the country. It has a membership of some 16 million in America, with some 42,000 churches. In a statement of its beliefs it insists that salvation is possible only through belief in Jesus Christ and his death on the Cross, and is predicated on baptism in the Christian church.

Non-Christians, no matter if they have led morally upright lives, 'become transgressors' and 'are under condemnation, that is, they are lost'.

Non-Christians, no matter if they have led morally upright lives, 'become transgressors' and 'are under condemnation, that is, they are lost'. It insists that those 'without a personal commitment to Jesus Christ will be consigned to a literal hell, the place of everlasting separation from God'. The SBC, like other evangelicals, sees as its primary task the conversion of the entire world to Christianity. 'The Great Commission mandate of our Lord Jesus', it declares, 'compels us to disciple the nations' (SBC Resolution on the Priority of Global Evangelism and Missions, 1999). In 2003 its overseas church membership stood at more than 7 million, with 1523 international missionaries working in the field.

Bush, for his part, has made no bones about his sympathies for the SBC. In 2002 he delivered an address to the SBC's annual convention through satellite, where he explicitly acknowledged the role of preachers of the SBC in 'nurturing' his 'faith'. He indicated in no uncertain terms his support to the SBC and its agenda by declaring, 'You and I share common commitments', including 'protecting human dignity' and 'human rights'. He ended his speech by thanking the SBC for what he called its 'good works'. 'You're believers, and you're patriots, faithful followers of God and good citizens of America', he said in closing, beseeching God to bless them and America.

Leading evangelicals have issued statements that clearly indicate that they see America as engaged in nothing less than a crusade against the Muslim world.

As an ultra-right wing church, the SBC's political stance has consistently been pro-establishment, and one of its principal functions has been to provide suitable theological sanction to American imperialism. In the heydays of the Soviet Union, the SBC was regarded as a bulwark against what was seen as the menacing threat of communism. It lent full support to the American state's war on communism, which it equated, in its own words, with 'cancer'. The 'Christian faith', it declared, 'is incompatible with communism'. It expressed its gratitude to 'all agencies, organizations and persons who guard our homes, our churches and our nation against communist subversion'. 'We speak our No to communism when we say Yes to Jesus Christ', it announced in a resolution passed at its annual meeting in 1962 at the height of the Cold War. It insisted that the 'proper and only adequate response to the challenge of communism is to be thoroughly Christian, and to seek to establish and support New Testament churches at home and abroad'.

The Crusade Against Islam

This, of course, tied in comfortably with the American policy of sponsoring right-wing Christian groups in the so-called 'Third World' to counter 'red menace'. Following the collapse of the Soviet Union, American Christian evangelicals have been among the most forceful champions of the Huntingtonian thesis of a 'clash of civilisations' pitting the 'Christian' West against Islam. Leading evangelicals have issued statements that clearly indicate that they see America as engaged in nothing less than a crusade against the Muslim world. No sooner had Bush announced America's latest imperialist offensive in Iraq (which he termed as a 'crusade') than the SBC rallied behind him to provide his declaration with religious sanction. At its annual meeting in 2002 the SBC passed a lengthy resolution on the 'war on terrorism', exhorting Christians to rally behind Bush. It enthusiastically blessed American imperialist aggression against Iraq by arguing that the Christian scriptures explicitly 'command civil authorities to restrain evil and to punish evildoers through the power of the sword'. It fervently appealed to Christians to 'pray for those in authority', and applauded what it called the 'moral clarity' of Bush in his denunciation of 'terrorist' groups as 'evildoers'. It resolved to 'wholeheartedly support the United States government, its intelligence agencies and its military' in what it called the 'just war' against the 'terrorist networks'. But, as it saw it, the war, while necessary, was not the final solution to the problem of 'terrorism', which could only come about through the global spread of Christianity. Hence, it concluded its resolution by insisting that the 'conversion of the people of all nations to salvation through belief in the Lord Jesus Christ' was 'the only ultimate answer to all forms of terrorism'.

An Historic Connection

The 2002 meeting of the SBC also passed an important resolution on the situation in West Asia. Like most other American evangelicals, and following faithfully the official American line, it expressed unstinted support for Israel. It insisted that the Old and the New Testaments 'affirm God's special purposes and providential care for the Jewish people', and argued that 'The Jewish people have an historic connection to the land of Israel, a connection that is rooted in the promises of God Himself'. It declared, in no uncertain terms, that Israel properly belonged to the Jews, claiming that the 'international community' had 'restored' land to the Jewish people in 1947 in order to 'provide a homeland for them and to re-establish the nation of Israel'. No mention, of course, was made of the forcible occupation at the land by the Zionists and the consequent killings and forced migrations of thousands of Palestinians, both Muslims and Christians. In a thinly veiled reference to Palestinian resistance to Israeli occupation it expressed its 'abhorrence of all forms of terrorism as inexcusable, barbaric and cowardly'. It provided 'Christian' sanction for denying the Palestinians the right to oppose the Israelis ('We denounce revenge in any form as a response to past offences', the resolution read), but at the same time asserted that Israel had the alleged God-given right to oppose the Palestinian resistance ('[We] support the right of sovereign nations to use force to defend themselves against aggressors'). In sort, it parroted what seems to be the standard American and Israeli line on the Palestinian issue.

The SBC is just one of a vast number of well-heeled American fundamentalist Christian organsations that are today major players in American domestic politics and exercise a powerful influence in shaping American foreign policies. The silence of the Western media, by and large, on their pernicious [hurtful, causing harm] theology and their backing for Western imperialism is hardly surprising, given that the entire onus for the deteriorating relations between the 'West' and the 'Muslim world' is consciously sought to be placed solely on the onus of the Muslims themselves. Clearly, if at all the 'clash of civilisations' thesis is to be prevented from coming true and leading the world to the brink of Armageddon, Christian fundamentalist imperialism cannot be left unchallenged.

Organizations to Contact

The editors have compiled the following list of organizations concerned with the issues debated in this book. The descriptions are derived from materials provided by the organizations. All have publications or information available for interested readers. The list was compiled on the date of publication of the present volume; the information provided here may change. Be aware that many organizations take several weeks or longer to respond to inquiries, so allow as much time as possible.

American Civil Liberties Union (ACLU)
125 Broad St., 18th Floor, New York, NY 10004
Web site: www.aclu.org

The ACLU is a large national organization that works to preserve First Amendment rights—freedom of speech, freedom of association and assembly, freedom of the press, and freedom of religion supported by the strict separation of church and state—as well as the right to equal protection under the law regardless of race, sex, religion, or national origin. Its Web site offers many articles, and it can be contacted for more information through online forms.

Americans for Religious Liberty
PO Box 6656, Silver Spring, MD 20916
(301) 260-2988 • fax: (301) 260-2989
e-mail: arlinc@verizon.net
Web site: www.arlinc.org

The mission of Americans for Religious Liberty is to defend the core constitutional principle of separation of church and state. In its quarter century of activism in defense of church-state separation and freedom of conscience, it has been involved in more than sixty actions in the courts. Its Web site offers articles, plus many print publications that can be purchased by mail.

Americans United for Separation of Church and State (AU)

518 C St. NE, Washington, DC   20002
(202) 466-3234 • fax: (202) 466-2587
e-mail: americansunited@au.org
Web site: www.au.org

Americans United is an independent nonprofit organization that protects separation of church and state by working on a wide range of pressing political and social issues. As a nonsectarian, nonpartisan organization, AU's membership includes Christians, Jews, Buddhists, people with no religious affiliation, and others. It publishes the monthly magazine *Church & State*, containing detailed articles about court cases and other news concerning religious liberty, of which archives are available at its Web site.

Brookings Institution

1775 Massachusetts Ave. NW, Washington, DC   20036
(202) 797-6000 • fax: (202) 797-6004
e-mail: communications@brookings.edu
Web site: www.brookings.edu

The Brookings Institution is a think tank conducting research and education in foreign policy, economics, government, and the social sciences. Publications include the quarterly *Brooking Review* and periodic *Policy Briefs*.

Dignity USA

PO Box 376, Medford, MA   02155
(800) 877-8797 • fax: (781) 397-0584
e-mail: info@dignityusa.org
Web site: www.dignityusa.org

Dignity USA is a Catholic organization of gay, lesbian, bisexual, and transgender (GLBT) persons who worship together and advocate for increased GLBT rights within the official church and in American society. *Breath of the Spirit* is a weekly electronic newsletter made available to members and friends of Dignity USA.

Family Research Council

810 G St. NW, Washington, DC 20001
(202) 393-2100 • fax: (202) 393-2134
Web site: www.frc.org

The Family Research Council is a research, resource, and education organization that promotes traditional marriage and traditional family structure as the foundations of a healthy and moral civilization. The organization also believes that the government has a duty to promote and protect traditional marriage in law and public policy. The organization's publications include *Getting It Straight: What the Research Shows about Homosexuality; The Bible, the Church, and Homosexuality*; and *Protecting Your Child in an X-Rated World*.

Focus on the Family

8655 Explorer Dr., Colorado Springs, CO 80920
(719) 531-5181 • fax: (719) 531-3424
e-mail: info@family.org
Web site: www.family.org

Focus on the Family is a conservative Christian organization that promotes traditional marriage and Bible-based perspectives on moral issues as part of its larger mission of evangelism. It also actively campaigns against abortion, homosexuality, pornography, sexual activity outside of traditional marriage, divorce, and other perceived threats to Christian society. Publications include the *Focus on the Family Marriage Series, A Parents' Guide to Preventing Homosexuality, And the Bride Wore White*, and *Why You Can't Stay Silent: A Biblical Mandate to Shape Our Culture*.

Heritage Foundation

214 Massachusetts Ave. NE, Washington, DC 20002-4999
(202) 546-4400 • fax: (202) 546-8328
e-mail: info@heritage.org
Web site: www.heritage.org

Founded in 1973, the Heritage Foundation is a conservative research and educational institute, whose mission is to formulate and promote conservative public policies based on the principles of free enterprise, limited government, and individual freedom. It publishes many books on foreign and domestic policy and religious freedom.

Institute for Policy Studies (IPS)

1112 16th St. NW, Suite 600, Washington, DC   20036
(202) 234-9382 • fax: (202) 387-7915
e-mail: info@ips-dc.org
Web site: www.ips-dc.org

The IPS is a progressive think tank working to develop societies built around the values of justice and nonviolence. It publishes reports, including *Global Perspectives: A Media Guide to Foreign Policy Experts*. Articles also are available online.

Institute on Religion and Public Policy

1620 I St. NW, Suite LL10, Washington, DC   20006
(202) 833-4777 • fax: (202) 833-2778
e-mail: irpp@religionandpolicy.org
Web site: www.religionandpolicy.org

The Institute on Religion and Public Policy is an international, interreligious, nonprofit organization dedicated to ensuring freedom of religion as the foundation for security, stability, and democracy. It works globally with government policy makers, religious leaders, nongovernmental organizations, and others to develop, protect, and promote fundamental rights—especially the right of religious freedom. Its Web site contains information about programs with which it is involved.

North American Religious Liberty Association (NARLA)

12501 Old Columbia Pike, Silver Spring, MD   20904
(301) 680-6685
e-mail: narla@religiousliberty.info
Web site: http://religiousliberty.info

NARLA, which is affiliated with the Seventh-day Adventist Church, exists to ensure that people of faith are accorded the fundamental right not only to hold their beliefs but to actively practice their faith. It also works to ensure that religion is not co-opted by the state through direct regulation or through financial control. It publishes the monthly magazine *Liberty*, containing articles about religious freedom; archives are available at www.libertymagazine.org.

Pew Forum on Religion & Public Life

1615 L St. NW, Suite 700, Washington, DC   20036
(202) 419-4550 • fax: (202) 419-4559
Web site: http://pewforum.org

The Pew Forum on Religion & Public Life in a nonpartisan, nonadvocacy organization that seeks to promote a deeper understanding of issues at the intersection of religion and public affairs. It pursues its mission by delivering timely, impartial information to national opinion leaders, including government officials and journalists, but does not take positions on policy debates. At its Web site there are many surveys and event transcripts as well as publications, and it also offers both an e-mail newsletter and an RSS news feed.

Soulforce

PO Box 3195, Lynchburg, VA   24503-0195
e-mail: info@soulforce.org
Web site: www.soulforce.org

Soulforce's mandate is to help lesbian, gay, bisexual, and transgender people gain greater freedom from perceived persecution at the hands of conservative religious people who, according to the organization, misuse religion to oppress homosexuals. Publications offered by Soulforce include *Religion Gone Bad: The Hidden Dangers of the Christian Right*, *Christian Youth: An Important Voice in the Present Struggle for Gay Rights in America*, and *What the Bible Says—and Doesn't Say—About Homosexuality*.

Bibliography

Books

Catherine Albanese — *A Republic of Mind and Spirit: A Cultural History of American Metaphysical Religion*. New Haven, CT: Yale University Press, 2007.

Scott Appleby, Gabriel Abraham Almond, and Emmanuel Sivan — *Strong Religion*. Chicago: University of Chicago Press, 2003.

Randall Herbert Balmer — *Mine Eyes Have Seen the Glory: A Journey into the Evangelical Subculture in America*, 4th ed. New York: Oxford University Press, 2006.

Craig Bartholomew, Jonathan Chaplin, and Al Wolters, eds. — *A Royal Priesthood: The Use of the Bible Ethically and Politically*. Grand Rapids, MI: Zondervan, 2002.

Amy Black, Douglas Koopman, and David Ryden — *Of Little Faith: The Politics of George W. Bush's Faith-Based Initiatives*. Washington, DC: Georgetown University Press, 2004.

Earl Black and Merle Black — *The Rise of Southern Republicans*. New York: Belknap/Harvard, 2002.

Gary Cox *Think Again: A Response to Fundamentalism's Claim on Christianity*. Wichita, KS: University Congregational Press, 2006.

Carlene Cross *Fleeing Fundamentalism: A Minister's Wife Examines Faith*. Chapel Hill, NC: Algonquin Books of Chapel Hill, 2006.

Edward Curtis *Black Muslim Religion in the Nation of Islam, 1960–1975*. Chapel Hill, NC: University of North Carolina Press, 2006.

John DiIulio Jr. *Godly Republic: A Centrist Blueprint for America's Faith-Based Future*. Berkeley, CA: University of California Press, 2007.

E.J. Dionne Jr. and Ming Hsu Chen, eds. *Sacred Places, Civic Purposes: Should Government Help Faith-Based Charity?* Washington, DC: The Brookings Institution, 2001.

C.J. Eberle *Religious Convictions in Liberal Politics*. Washington, DC: Catholic University Press, 2002.

Kathleen Flake *The Politics of American Religious Identity: The Seating of Senator Reed Smoot, Mormon Apostle*. Chapel Hill, NC: University of North Carolina Press, 2004.

Richard Wightman Fox *Jesus in America: Personal Savior, Cultural Hero, National Obsession*. San Francisco: HarperCollins, 2004.

Thomas Frank

What's the Matter with Kansas?: How Conservatives Won the Heart of America. New York: Metropolitan Books, 2004.

Philip Goff and Paul Harvey, eds.

Themes in Religion and American Culture. Chapel Hill, NC: University of North Carolina Press, 2004.

Paul Grieve

A Brief Guide to Islam: History, Faith and Politics: The Complete Introduction. New York: Carroll and Graf Publishers, 2006.

Chris Hedges

American Fascists: The Christian Right and the War on America. New York: Free Press, 2007.

James Hudnut-Beumier

In Pursuit of the Almighty's Dollar: A History of Money and American Protestantism. Chapel Hill, NC: University of North Carolina Press, 2007.

Esther Kaplan

With God on Their Side: How Christian Fundamentalists Trampled Science, Policy, and Democracy in George W. Bush's White House. New York: The New Press, 2004.

Carl Kell, ed.

Exiled: Voices of the Southern Baptist Convention Holy War. Knoxville, TN: University of Tennessee Press, 2006.

Douglas Laycock Jr., et al., eds.

Same-Sex Marriage and Religious Liberty: Emerging Conflicts. Lanham, MD: Rowman & Littlefield Publishers, 2008.

Camille Kaminski Lewis — *Romancing the Difference: Kenneth Burke, Bob Jones University, and the Rhetoric of Religious Fundamentalism.* Waco, TX: Baylor University Press, 2007.

George Marsden — *Fundamentalism and American Culture.* New York: Oxford University Press, 2006.

Paul Marshall — *God and the Constitution.* Lanham, MD: Rowman & Littlefield Publishers, 2002.

Kevin Phillips — *American Theocracy: The Peril and Politics of Radical Religion, Oil, and Borrowed Money in the 21st Century.* New York: Penguin Group, 2006.

Stephen Prothero, ed. — *A Nation of Religions: The Politics of Pluralism in Multireligious America.* Chapel Hill, NC: University of North Carolina Press, 2006.

Olivier Roy — *Secularism Confronts Islam.* New York: Columbia University Press, 2007.

Malise Ruthven — *Fundamentalism: The Search for Meaning.* Oxford, United Kingdom: Oxford University Press, 2005.

B. Sammon — *The Evangelical President: George Bush's Struggle to Spread a Moral Democracy Throughout the World.* Washington, DC: Regnery Publishing, 2007.

Earl Shorris   *The Politics of Heaven: America in Fearful Times.* New York: Norton, 2007.

Peter Singer   *The President of Good and Evil: The Ethics of George W. Bush.* New York: Dutton/Plume, 2004.

Gary Scott Smith   *Faith and the Presidency: From George Washington to George W. Bush.* New York: Oxford University Press, 2006.

Periodicals

M. Russell Ballard   "What Matters Most Is What Lasts Longest," *Ensign*, November 2005.

David Bukay   "Peace or Jihad? Abrogation in Islam," *Middle East Quarterly*, Fall 2007.

Daily Herald   "Could Abe Honestly Win in Today's Religion-Packed Vote?" March 1, 2008.

Ross Douthat   "Theocracy, Theocracy, Theocracy," *First Things: A Monthly Journal of Religion and Public Life*, August 2006.

Maggie Gallagher   "Banned in Boston: The Coming Conflict Between Same-Sex Marriage and Religious Liberty," *The Weekly Standard*, May 15, 2006.

Paul Lauritzen   "Holy Alliance? the Danger of Mixing Politics & Religion," *Commonweal*, March 24, 2006.

Ira Lupu and Robert Tuttle — "The Faith-Based Initiative and the Constitution," *DePaul Law Review*, 2005.

Andrew Murphy — "The Founding Fathers and the Place of Religion in America," *The Christian Century*, February 24, 2004.

Richard John Neuhaus — "Dechristianizing America," *First Things: A Monthly Journal of Religion and Public Life*, June 2006.

Richard John Neuhaus — "America, Islam, and a Somewhat More Peaceful World," *First Things: A Monthly Journal of Religion and Public Life*, August 2007.

David Niose — "The Stillborn God: Religion, Politics, and the Modern West," *The Humanist*, January 2008.

David Novak — "Theology, Politics, and Abraham Joshua Heschel," *First Things: A Monthly Journal of Religion and Public Life*, February 2008.

Ramesh Ponnuru — "Secularism and Its Discontents: The Debate over Religion and Politics Is in Desperate Need of Sanity," *National Review*, December 27, 2004.

David Saperstein — "Public Values in an Era of Privatization: Public Accountability and Faith-Based Organizations: A Problem Best Avoided," *Harvard Law Review*, 2003.

Gary Taylor and Helen Hawley — "Freedom of Religion in America," *Contemporary Review*, June 2003.

Bassam Tibi	"The Totalitarianism of Jihadist Islamism and Its Challenge to Europe and to Islam," *Totalitarian Movements and Political Religions*, March 2007.
Christine Vestal	"California Gay Marriage Ruling Sparks New Debate," *Stateline.org*, May 16, 2008.
The Washington Times	"Anti-War Protestants; the Fusion of Left-Wing Politics and Religion," April 21, 2003.
The Washington Times	"'U.S. Should Be Open to God's Priorities;' Bush Touts Religion in Politics at Prayer Breakfast," February 4, 2005.
The Washington Times	"Politics, Not Religion," December 7, 2005.
David Westbrook	"America the Comfortable," *First Things: A Monthly Journal of Religion and Public Life*, March 2006.
Anne Blue Wills	"The Politics of Heaven: America in Fearful Times," *The Christian Century*, July 15, 2008.

Index